Atlantic and Danville Railway Company

the Railroad of Southside Virginia

Revised and Expanded Second Edition

THE ATLANTIC & DANVILLE RAILWAY COMPANY

A&D

TLC Publishing, Inc. 2006

By William E. Griffin, Jr.

FOREWORD/ACKNOWLEDGEMENTS

The first edition of my book on the Atlantic and Danville was published in 1986 and sold out almost immediately. I sincerely appreciate that TLC Publishing has allowed me to republish this expanded second edition which updates the history of the railroad since 1986 and incorporates much material not available to me when the book was first published.

Originally chartered in 1882 as a narrow gauge railroad, a 50-mile line of 3-foot gauge track was completed from Claremont on the James River to Belfield (now Emporia) in 1885. The ambitions of its builders expanded and the company was reincorporated in 1886 with authority to move the principal deep water terminus to the Norfolk area and then to construct a standard gauge railroad west to Danville by way of a connection with the narrow gauge line near Belfield at James River Junction.

This narrow gauge line, mainly built with capital derived from county subscriptions, was thereafter relegated to branch line status. Construction of the standard gauge line, accomplished by means of a large investment of English capital, quickly drove the company into bankruptcy and receivership. This receivership led to a reorganization in 1894 and the railroad came under the control of its English investors.

In 1899, the A&D's English owners leased the entire railroad to the Southern Railway for a period of 50 years. During the term of the lease, the Southern Railway gradually reduced the through freight service over the A&D favoring instead to operate into the Norfolk area via trackage rights over the Atlantic Coast Line Railroad's route from Selma, North Carolina.

When the Southern elected not to renew the lease, the A&D's second period of independent operation began on August 1, 1949. It ended in 1962 when the company's assets were purchased by the Norfolk and Western Railway and the property was renamed the Norfolk, Franklin and Danville Railway.

A large portion of the NF&D was abandoned after the N&W/Southern merger and creation of the Norfolk Southern Corporation in 1982. The railroad finally lost its separate corporate identity when absorbed into the N&W in December of 1983.

The author wishes to acknowledge that this book would not have been possible without the contributions of many people. I am especially indebted to F. Edward "Ed" Sharpe and James M. King for their friendship and continuing assistance. Both are longtime A&D fans and James is the founder and president of the Atlantic and Danville Railway Historical Society. They were always there to help seek out essential facts and Ed often contacted former employees for their first-hand recollections. I am also indebted in this second edition for information on A&D and NF&D rolling stock provided by Russell Underwood, who has become an authority on the subject.

I am also particularly grateful for the important assistance given by my friends G. W. "Bill" Schafer and R. H. "Bob" Whitaker, who shared their files on the Southern Railway; Carl W. Shaver of the Chesapeake and Ohio Railway Historical Society who helped with Equipment Registers; James A. McGhee, curator of the Old Smoky Railway Museum for much station data; Oscar W. Kimsey, who enabled the author to obtain the many station photos found in this second edition; Frank Malone, Executive Director of the South Hill Chamber of Commerce; the staff of the South Hill Railroad Museum; my cousin Stanley W. Short, another longtime A&D fan; Michael P. Casen; James E. "Jim" King, III; D. Wallace Johnson; and Donald P. Traser. They each provided help and encouragement throughout the project.

Thanks is also extended to former A&D/NF&D employees J. W. Browder, Jr., T. A. "Ted" Eudy, Maddux Earl Short, W. C. Market, Mack R. Ballance and Fitzhugh Ritt for their assistance.

Finally, the author is grateful to the many photographers and collectors who have enriched this book by making photographs available from their collections. While each photograph has been individually credited, I would nevertheless like to acknowledge with deep appreciation the assistance of : Curt Tillotson, Jr.; H. Reid; Wiley M. Bryan; August A. Thieme, Jr.; Shelby F. Lowe; William B. Gwaltney; H. D. Conner; Bob Lorenz; R. E. "Ed" Fielding; Jim Shaw; Warren Calloway; John F. Gilbert; Ed Sharpe; James M. King; Harold K. Vollrath; Thomas G. Moore; Tom G. King; C. K. Marsh, Jr.; Tom L. Sink; Bob Graham; the Mariners Museum of Newport News, Virginia; J. D. Thompson of Alco Historical Photos; J. W. Browder, Jr.; Ted Eudy; Tal Carey; Stanley W. Short; my brother D. Courtney Griffin; Thomas G. Wicker; the Virginia State Library; Mallory Hope Ferrell; L. D. Moore, Jr.; Jacqueline Hudson Wheeler; Ralph Coleman; J. Parker Lamb; Thomas Norrell; Robert G. Lewis; Fred Mullins; Russell Underwood; Frank E. Ardrey, Jr.; Russell Wayne Davis; Jack Huber; H. T. Crittenden; W. C. Whittaker; C. L. Goolsby; John P. Stith; William G. McClure; Jack Bruce; and, Charles McIntyre.

William E. Griffin, Jr.
Orange Park, Florida

April 1, 2004

DEDICATION

This book is dedicated to the memory of the author's nephew, Thomas Clayton Griffin. He died on July 29, 1984 at age 12 - a victim of the genetic disease cystic fibrosis.

Clay was a complete railfan and his love of trains sustained him through a life of daily struggles against the effects of the disease. He was witty and gifted and the most courageous person I have ever known.

TABLE OF CONTENTS

International Standard Book Number: 0-9766201-3-8
Design & Layout by
Megan Johnson
Johnson2Design, Rustburg, VA

Printed in USA
by Walsworth Publishing Co., Marceline, MO

CHAPTER 1

THE EARLY YEARS - BUILDING THE MAIN LINE
1882-1899

The Atlantic and Danville Railway Company was incorporated by an act of the General Assembly of the Commonwealth of Virginia on April 21, 1882. The Company's charter authorized construction of a narrow gauge (three foot) railroad "... from the most available point at deep water, on the James River, within the County of Surry, and passing through or near the Town of Waverly, Sussex County, thence by the most direct and practicable route, to a point at or near the Town of Belfield, Greensville County; thence by the most practicable route, to a point near Brunswick Courthouse; thence by the most practicable route to a point at or near Boydton, County of Mecklenburg, then by the most practicable route, to a point at or near the City of Danville".

The 50-mile 3-foot narrow gauge line from Claremont to Emporia was the first portion of the railroad built pursuant to the original charter of the Atlantic and Danville Railway. Following the re-incorporation of the A&D in 1886 to operate between Norfolk and Danville, it was thereafter operated as a narrow gauge branch line of the standard gauge railroad. This map of the Claremont Branch, dated June 27, 1932, shows the connecting rail lines and intersecting highways at the time of the abandonment of the line. (William E. Griffin, Jr. Collection)

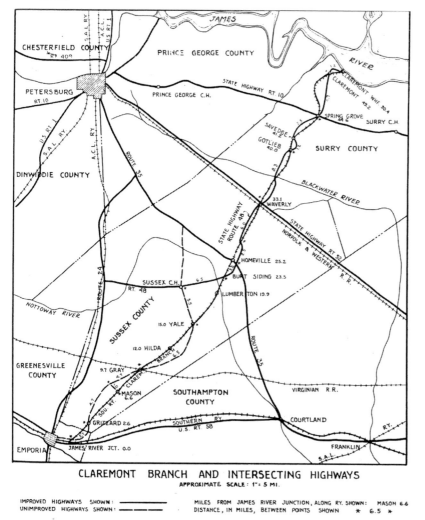

CLAREMONT BRANCH AND INTERSECTING HIGHWAYS
APPROXIMATE SCALE : 1"= 5 MI.

IMPROVED HIGHWAYS SHOWN : ———————
UNIMPROVED HIGHWAYS SHOWN : ------------

MILES FROM JAMES RIVER JUNCTION, ALONG RY. SHOWN : MASON 6.6
DISTANCE , IN MILES, BETWEEN POINTS SHOWN   * 6.5 *

A-4304   June 27 1932

Interestingly, that very same day the legislature also granted a charter to another railroad for the construction of a rail line from some point on the James River into Surry County. However, this railroad, known as the Surry County Railroad and Lumber Company, was originally intended to be nothing more than a tramway for the transportation of timber between Sloop Point on the James River and the lumber mill of David Steele at Mussel Fork.

The founders of the Atlantic and Danville had a bolder dream. They envisioned that their line would be part of a chain of railroads that would pass through Danville, then extend westward to capture a portion of the traffic collected in the Midwest by the North's big rail systems. Pamphlets published to promote construction of the A&D pointed out that the new railroad would give Danville an independent and competing line to deep water. At that time, the nearest route was via the Richmond & Danville and Norfolk & Western railroads to Norfolk, a distance of 220 miles. The A&D's route to a deep water terminal on the James River would be but 155 miles and over supposedly easier grades. The pamphlets also boasted that the Danville and New River Railroad would be built westward from Danville and that the two railroads would "... connect at Danville and be practically one line".

The A&D was organized on December 2, 1882 and, pursuant to a provision in its charter, the principal office was located at Waverly, Virginia. A resident of Waverly - John M. Bailey - was elected by the Board of Directors to serve as the company's first president. The composition of this first board evidenced the local influence and control over the railroad. In addition to Bailey, it included Virginians' P. Fleetwood of Waverly, Benjamin D. Tiller of Hicksford and Cicero Burruss of Norfolk. The lone northerner was Henry L. Ballow of Woonsocket, Rhode Island.

The A&D selected Claremont, which was located approximately a mile and a half down the river from the Surry County Railroad and Lumber Company's wharf at Sloop Point, to serve as its James River terminus. Construction of the railroad southward from Claremont commenced on April 2, 1883.

At the same time, the Surry County Railroad and Lumber Company had been progressing the construction of its rail line in a northward direction from the Surry Lumber Company's Mussel Forks Mill on the Blackwater River. The tracks of the two companies would share the same trackage between that point and Claremont. This arrangement continued until May 26, 1886, then the lumber company decided to build its own rail line and reorganized the Surry County Railroad and Lumber Company to form the Surry, Sussex and Southampton Railroad.

Capital for the construction of the A&D was

1

This builder's photograph shows the original appearance of A&D narrow gauge 2-6-0 No. 2, built at the Rhode Island Works of the American Locomotive Company in 1886. When the A&D was acquired by the Southern Railway, it was renumbered the N-2 by the Southern and continued to work on the Claremont Branch until retired and scrapped at Spencer, North Carolina in 1934. (Alco Historic Photos)

largely derived from county subscriptions authorized by the railroad's charter. Under the charter, the counties through which the line would pass could subscribe to the capital stock of the railroad up to the amount of $3,500 per mile for each mile of railroad to be constructed within the county. The subscriptions by the counties were conditioned upon the railroad actually being built and were payable when a county commissioner certified that one or more miles of track had been graded and laid in his county. Capital was also derived from the sale of 6% bonds, issued at the rate of $8,000 per mile of road, and secured under a first mortgage dated October 1, 1883.

By September of 1883, 14 miles of track had been completed at an estimated cost of $15,000 per mile. The three-foot gauge line, laid with 30 to 40 pound steel rail, reached Waverly before the end of the year. During this period, the A&D had not been opened for business, its operations confined entirely to the transportation of construction material.

The A&D had hoped to reach Belfield in August of 1884, but it encountered difficulties that stalled the progress of construction. Early in 1884, the company was required to go back to the General Assembly for an amendment of its charter to authorize the construction of wharves at Claremont and to increase the capital stock. That capital proved to be difficult to raise because by mid-year a declining stock market had pushed the nation's economy into a recession. The A&D found it necessary to again return to the legislature when it was unable to prosecute construction through Sussex and Greensville counties as prescribed in its charter. By an act approved on November 22, 1884, authority was obtained for certain minor modifications of the original route.

The country's economy recovered quickly in 1885 and the A&D completed another 40 miles of rail line during the year, reaching Hicksford in October and Belfield in December. Belfield was also served by the Petersburg Railroad Company, a predecessor of the Atlantic Coast Line Railroad Company that operated south of Petersburg, Virginia to Weldon, North Carolina. The area prospered and Hicksford and Belfield were later incorporated into a new town named Emporia.

The A&D commenced revenue operation in 1885 and the report of the Virginia Railroad Commissioner for the year showed the company owned 2 locomotives, 7 first-class passenger cars, 2 baggage, mail and express cars, and 68 freight cars. The report defined a "first-class" car as one having eight wheels.

In 1885, the A&D moved its principal office from Waverly

to Hicksford and Benjamin D. Tiller, a resident of Hicksford, succeeded Cicero Burruss as president. Burruss, a resident of Norfolk, had served as president during 1884. During this early period of the A&D's history, the members of the Board of Directors remained substantially unchanged but pursuant to a provision in the charter, the board elected a new president each year.

With operations established between Claremont and Belfield, the A&D made its plans to construct the proposed extension to Danville. Those plans would involve additional amendments to the company's charter because the A&D management had determined to make Norfolk, rather than Claremont, the deep water terminus and to construct the line to Danville of standard gauge rather than narrow gauge. By act of the General Assembly approved February 24, 1886, the A&D's charter was amended to authorize the company to build " ... a railway, either of standard or narrow gauge, and may change the gauge of the road already built ..." and to "... operate its railway from any point on its main line, east of the town of Hicksford ... to a point on the Elizabeth River, either in or near the City of Norfolk, or in or near the City of Portsmouth ..."

The A&D's decision to build its line to Danville with standard gauge was consistent with the adoption of a uniform gauge by other southern railroads in the late 1880's. At the beginning of the decade, there had been fourteen different broad gauges and seven different narrow gauges in operation, with over 80 percent of southern trackage of a five-foot gauge. However, between 1885 and 1886, most of the southern railroads changed to the English standard gauge of 4 feet, 8 1/2 inches to facilitate the interchange of traffic with the northern railroads. The A&D never rebuilt the Claremont to Belfield line to standard gauge and in the years to follow it was known as the James River Division, a narrow gauge branch line of the standard gauge railroad.

The A&D's decision to change its deep water terminus from Claremont to Norfolk also must be viewed in the historical context of the period. For more than one hundred years Virginia's fall-line ports such as Richmond on the James River and Petersburg on the Appomattox River had prospered as trade centers. However, as ocean vessels increased in size, it became increasingly difficult for them to come up the rivers. Also, the light draft

With the exception of one 0-4-0 and one 2-6-0, all of the standard gauge steam locomotives operated by the A&D were 4-4-0 type locomotives such as No. 23, shown here in an 1890 builder' photograph. Built at the Richmond Locomotive Works, No. 23 passed to the Southern Railway under its lease of the A&D and was destroyed in an accident at M. P. 69 (near James River Junction) on October 19, 1903. (Alco Historic Photos)

vessels that could come up the rivers were unable to compete with the larger steamboats for foreign trade. Trade via the rivers was in steep decline and by the mid-1880's, Norfolk had replaced her rivals as the principal deep water port in Virginia.

The A&D began construction of its standard gauge line from Hicksford westward to Danville in January of 1887. During the year, the A&D also established a deep water terminal at West Norfolk on the Elizabeth River and began construction of a standard gauge line from that point toward Hicksford. By April, the A&D had built about seven miles of line from West Norfolk to a point known as Shoulders Hill.

The funds for the main line construction were derived in part from municipal subscriptions, but chiefly from the sale of company bonds secured under a first mortgage dated September 7, 1887 to Mercantile Trust Company of New York City. Under this mortgage the A&D issued $4,952,000 of 6 percent bonds at the rate of $16,000 per mile of road constructed. However, with the acquisition of northern capital to finance the construction project, control of the company by local interests was lost. Of the five members of the A&D Board of Directors elected at the 1887 stockholders' meeting, four were New Yorkers. Thomas Ewing, a resident of the City of New York, was elected President and Chairman of the Board.

During 1887, the A&D also moved its principal office from Hicksford to Portsmouth. After the A&D completed that portion of the new line between West Norfolk and Shoulders Hill, it entered into negotiations with the City of Portsmouth for construction of a rail line into that city. On September 7, 1887, in consideration of the city agreeing to subscribe for $150,000 of the capital stock of the company, the A&D agreed to lay tracks from Shoulders Hill to the City of Portsmouth. The A&D also agreed to establish a terminal in the city on the property of the Seaboard Cotton Compress Company and to locate its general offices, freight and passenger depots, roundhouse, shops and freight yards, within or adjacent to the city. A referendum of the Portsmouth electorate approved the city's sale of bonds and the rail line was built.

The eventful year of 1887 also saw the A&D return to the Virginia legislature for yet another amendment to its charter. This act of the General Assembly, dated May 5, 1887, finally fixed the route of the line to Danville as it was eventually completed.

The A&D's main line was built following a route that had been awarded some years earlier to a proposed railroad named the Norfolk and Great Western. The Norfolk and Great Western had been chartered in February of 1867 to build a railroad between Norfolk and Danville, with an ultimate extension of the line to Bristol where it would con-

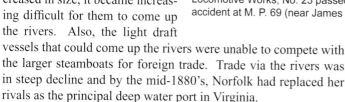

Locomotive Engineer J. J. Hinman (holding the oil can), Conductor Vanderson (wearing conductor's cap and uniform) and Porter and Brakeman Henry Newton (standing on the coach) join local residents to pose with their train at the Buffalo Lithia Springs health resort in a photograph taken circa 1890. The locomotive is A&D 4-4-0 No. 9, one of the railroad's original standard gauge engines. The resort was located on the Buffalo Springs branch line and during the "Gay Nineties", the A&D operated passenger trains six times daily between Buffalo Junction and the Springs during the peak season. Mecklenburg County had many mineral springs, the most famous being the Buffalo Springs, where the resort boasted that the waters "... burst forth from their hidden sources to gratify the thirst, and give relief, and brighten the life of afflicted humanity". (Shelby F. Lowe Collection)

ATLANTIC AND DANVILLE RAILWAY STANDARD GAUGE STEAM LOCOMOTIVES—1899

NUMBER	TYPE	CYLINDERS	BUILDER	DATE	DISPOSITION
8	4-4-0	15 × 20	Seaboard & Roanoke	1877	Condemned 6/1904
9	4-4-0	odd	unknown	1877	Condemned, Lawrenceville 12/31/1899
10	4-4-0	16 × 24	McQueen	unknown	Scrapped, Manchester 9/1909
11	4-4-0	odd	Cooke	unknown	Condemned, Lawrenceville 3/31/1901
12	4-4-0	unknown	Pittsburgh & Eastern	unknown	Condemned, Lawrenceville 1901
13	4-4-0	17 × 24	Baldwin	1889	Scrapped, Spencer 1/1922
14	4-4-0	17 × 24	Baldwin	1889	Scrapped, Sheffield 10/1933
15	4-4-0	16 × 22	Baldwin	1883	Sold, Consolidated Salvage 9/1923
16	0-4-0	16 × 22	Baldwin	1890	Scrapped, Lawrenceville 4/1912
17	4-4-0	17 × 24	Baldwin	1889	Scrapped, Manchester 1/1922
18	4-4-0	17 × 24	Baldwin	1889	Scrapped, Lawrenceville 1/1922
20	4-4-0	17 × 24	Richmond	1890	Scrapped, Lawrenceville 9/1909
21	4-4-0	17 × 24	Richmond	1890	Scrapped, Spencer 9/1909
22	4-4-0	17 × 24	Richmond	1890	Scrapped, Lawrenceville 10/1910
23	4-4-0	17 × 24	Richmond	1890	Destroyed, M.P. 69 Richmond Div. 10/19/1903
24	4-4-0	17 × 24	Pittsburgh	1889	Scrapped, Lawrenceville 1/1922
25	4-4-0	16 × 24	Grant	unknown	Scrapped, Lawrenceville 4/1914
26	2-6-0	17 × 24	Richmond	1888	Destroyed, Franklin, Va. 1/11/1904
27	4-4-0	17 × 24	Pittsburgh	1889	Scrapped, Lawrenceville 1/1922
28	4-4-0	17 × 24	Baldwin	1890	Scrapped, Spencer 1/1922
29	4-4-0	17 × 24	NYLW	1890	Scrapped, Lawrenceville 8/1911
30	4-4-0	17 × 24	Baldwin	1890	Scrapped, Lawrenceville 1/1922
32	4-4-0	odd	Baldwin	1869	Condemned, Lawrenceville 12/13/1899

A list of the standard gauge steam locomotives owned by the A&D at the time of its lease to the Southern Railway in 1899.

nect with other rail lines to the midwest and deep south. Surveys to Danville were completed by 1872. However, the railroad was never built as the counties and towns along its route were unable to subscribe to its stock. Their finances had not yet been straightened out form the entanglements of the War Between the States.

By December of 1887, the A&D was operating trains on the new main line between Portsmouth and Suffolk and on the West Norfolk branch, which connected with the main line at Shoulders Hill. Connection was made at Suffolk with the Suffolk and Carolina Railroad and for a brief period through passenger service was offered over the two railroads between Portsmouth and Chowan, North Carolina.

Construction of the main line was pushed westward from Suffolk in 1888, with the line opened to Franklin in May and connection made with the James River Division at Belfield in September. An A&D timetable for June 17, 1888 showed an eastbound passenger train leaving Jerusalem (now Courtland) at 5:40 a.m. and arriving at Portsmouth at 1:58 p.m. Another train left Franklin at 1:58 p.m. and arrived at Portsmouth at 5:00 p.m. Westbound trains arrived at Jerusalem at 1:06 p.m. and 7:20 p.m.

When the survey of the western portion of the main line was completed it was found that, because of the topography, it would be necessary for the line to dip into the State of North Carolina at several points. Thus, the A&D had to obtain a franchise from the State of North Carolina before it could build and operate its railroad in that state.

On December 1, 1888, the A&D filed Articles of Association under the state's general railroad law with the Secretary of the State of North Carolina. The authority for the A&D's right of way through the Carolina counties of Granville, Person and Caswell for a total length of about twenty miles was granted under a charter dated January 10, 1889.

Meanwhile, the construction of the railroad had been progressing slowly. It took almost eight months to complete the 14 miles of track between Belfield and Edgerton in Brunswick County. The line was opened to Lawrenceville on August 15, 1889.

Since Lawrenceville was situated approximately midway between Norfolk and Danville, it was chosen as the site for the A&D's shops and division headquarters. Two depots, one for passengers and another for freight, as well as a warehouse, car shops, water tank, carpentry shop, eight-stall roundhouse and turntable were located here. Lawrenceville became a railroad town and at one time the A&D employed over two hundred of its residents.

Building west from Lawrenceville, the pace of construction quickened. With its route firmly established and the necessary charter obtained from the State of North Carolina, the A&D vigorously pressed forward to reach Danville. All along its right-of-way new towns were established. Some of the new towns - such as Baskerville and South Hill - were actually laid out and surveyed by the financiers of the railroad, who also bought property around the town's depots.

In the vicinity of Clarksville, Virginia, the builders of the A&D made a decision to share approximately two miles of an existing railroad rather than build their own line. By agreement dated August 15, 1889, the Richmond and Danville Railroad granted the A&D the right to use the track and structures of the Richmond and Mecklenburg Railroad for a distance of 1.87 miles between Jeffress and Clarksville Junction. Under this agreement, the A&D was obligated to pay an annual rental of $4,125; one-half the cost of maintenance; and, to furnish the necessary operators and interlockings at each junction.

The Richmond and Mecklenburg Railroad Company had been incorporated in 1875 to build a 31-mile railroad from Keysville, on the Richmond and Danville Railroad, via Chase City to the Town of Clarksville. The Richmond and Mecklenburg was opened for operation in 1884 and by agreement dated November 21, 1888, it was leased to the Richmond and Danville. On July 1, 1894, the newly formed Southern Railway took over the Richmond and Danville by foreclosure and on November 1, 1898, it leased the Richmond and Mecklenburg for a term of 50 years.

In retrospect, the decision of the A&D to lease the use of the Richmond and Mecklenburg trackage appears quite strange. Perhaps the terms of the lease were more favorable than the projected construction costs. Perhaps the decision was motivated by the A&D's haste to complete the line to Danville and the company intended on building its own trackage at some later date. Whatever their original intentions, the A&D never joined the two segments of its railroad. Throughout the balance of its history, the A&D owned 140.5 miles of track between West Norfolk and Jeffress and 62.73 miles between Clarksville Junction and Danville. The only connection between the two segments was the 1.87 miles of Richmond and Mecklenburg trackage. This arrangement would be the source of controversy in the years ahead.

The tracks of the A&D were finally completed to Danville on February 15, 1890. Of course, the local newspapers reported the event with the usual hyperbolic and florid rhetoric that was so characteristic of their era. But it was a significant event as the A&D would provide the agricultural communities of Southside Virginia with their first rail link to a deep water port. Finally, the farmers of Southside had a road to the world market for their goods.

And the A&D that reached Danville was markedly changed from the little three-foot gauge railroad that had commenced construction at Claremont in 1883. The A&D of 1890 was a standard gauge railroad with 203 miles of main line from Portsmouth to Danville. Along the way, branch lines had been built from Shoulders Hill to the Elizabeth River terminal at West Norfolk (10.6 miles); from Atkins (now Buffalo Junction) to Colonel Thomas F. Goode's resort at Buffalo Lithia Springs (3.9 miles); from Emporia to the Hitchcock lumber mill (8.3 miles); and, from Beamon to a place known as Sleepy Hole (4 miles). The trackage from Claremont to Emporia was operated as a narrow gauge branch line (51 miles). The company had 27 steam locomotives; 22 passenger/baggage/express cars; 961 freight cars (338 box cars and 623 platform); 3 tugboats; 2 steamboats; 5 barges; and, over 900 employees.

However, the anticipated traffic failed to materialize and almost immediately the A&D was in financial difficulty. There was also a scandal concerning the construction expenditures for the main line. Writers of the day would say that the "work had not been done with economy".

The construction of the main line had been financed in part by means of a large investment of capital represented by Benjamin Newgass and Company of London, England. Newgass and Company were the largest holders of the A&D's bonds (over $3,000,000) and had advanced a substantial amount of money to the railroad to meet payroll expenses and other charges.

By the winter of 1890, the A&D's receipts were insufficient to pay the railroad's expenses and interest charges. Newgass took action to protect his company's investment.

On January 2, 1891, he obtained a confessed judgment against the A&D for advances made to the railroad totaling $362,839.

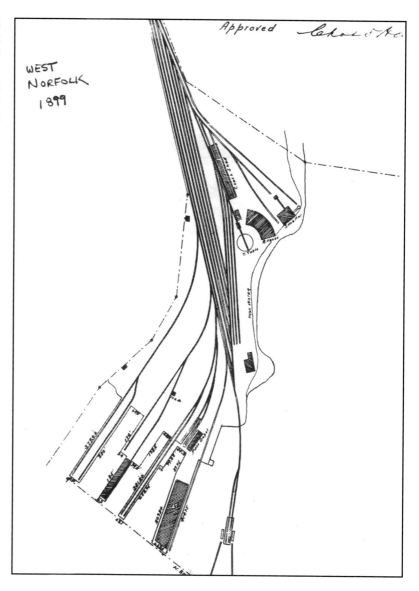

This diagram shows the substantial facilities operated by the A&D at its West Norfolk terminal in 1899. Terminal facilities included a coach shed, roundhouse, turntable, passenger depot and four piers with transfer bridges and trestles. (William E. Griffin, Jr. Collection)

Having obtained this judgment, Newgass and Company then instituted a suit against the A&D in the Circuit Court for the Eastern District of Virginia on January 3, 1891 to bring about a foreclosure sale of the property to satisfy their judgment and to have the railroad placed in the hands of a receiver. That same day, the court entered an order appointing Charles B. Cromwell and Alfred P. Thom as receivers.

In the meantime, the A&D had also defaulted on the payment of interest due on the bonds secured by the first mortgage to the Mercantile Trust Company. On January 7, 1891, Mercantile filed a petition with the Circuit Court to intervene in the Newgass suit and to foreclose its first mortgage of September 7, 1887.

Newgass and Mercantile were not the only creditors. During the years 1888 and 1889 the A&D, finding additional standard gauge rolling stock necessary as a result of its increased mileage, had made numerous purchases from car-equipment companies under car-trust contracts. During the period August 8, 1890 to January 13, 1891, the A&D issued collateral trust notes totaling over $300,000 in payment for equipment. These car-trust creditors also intervened in the bondholders' foreclosure suit asserting liens upon

ATLANTIC & DANVILLE RAILWAY.
DANVILLE SHORT LINE.
QUICKEST ROUTE TO
Atlanta, New Orleans, and the South.

TRAINS LEAVE WESTWARD.

Dist. Miles	STATIONS.	No. 1. Daily.	No. 3. Daily, except Sundays.	No. 5. Daily, except Sundays.
	Leave Norfolk	9.40 a.m.		
0	Leave Portsmouth	10.00 a.m.	3.15 p.m.	
3	Duncan	10.09	3.25	
5	Bunting	10.14	3.29	
6	Hodge's Ferry	10.17	3.34	
9½	Peake's Siding	10.22	3.38	
11	Shoulder's Hill	10.27	3.43	
14	Beamon	10.34	3.50	
16	Lindale	10.39	3.55	
20	Suffolk	10.49	4.07	
24	Manning	10.58	4.17	
27	Copeland	11.05	4.27	
29½	Daughtrey	11.10	4.33	
31	Holland	11.15	4.38	
34	Elwood	11.22	4.44	
36	Lee's Mill	11.31	4.55	
40	Franklin	11.38	5.02	
42½	Isaacs	11.43	5.07	
45½	Storys	11.50	5.12	
48	Courtland	11.59	5.20	
54	Pope	12.13 p.m.	5.34	
56	Capron	12.18	5.40	
62	Drewryville	12.32	5.59	
67	Adams' Grove	12.44	6.00	
70	Green Plains	12.51	6.16	
71	James River Junc.	12.54	6.23	
75	Helfield	1.05	6.35	
79	Durand	1.14	6.46	
83	Pleasant Shade	1.23	6.56	
89	Edgerton	1.43	7.14	
94	Lawrenceville	2.14	7.30	6.30 a.m.
107	Brodnax	2.50		7.03
111	La Crosse	2.53		7.06
114	South Hill	3.10		7.20
120	Union Level	3.30		7.35
124	Baskerville	3.39		7.42
128	Gills	3.42		7.46
131	Boydton	3.54		8.00
138	Finchley	4.08		8.14
141	Jeffress	4.16		8.24
143	Clarksville	4.24		8.33
149	Atkins	4.35		8.45
159	Virgilina	5.03		9.08
167	Mayo	5.21		9.27
170	Denniston Junction	5.32		9.40
172	Harmony	5.37		9.45
174	Alton	5.45		9.51
180	Cuningham	6.01		10.04
184	Semora	6.16		10.17
191	Milton	6.34		10.35
198	Blanche	6.45		10.51
205	Arrive Danville	7.10		11.10
	Arrive Greensboro (R. & D.)	10.20 p.m.		
	Charlotte	2.10 a.m.		
	Atlanta	1.15 p.m.		
	Montgomery (W. & Atl.)	8.10		
	Mobile (L. & N.)	2.05 a.m.		
	New Orleans	7.00		

Solid train Portsmouth to Danville.
Pullman Buffet Car Danville to Atlanta, and Atlanta to New Orleans without change.

ATLANTIC & DANVILLE RAILWAY.
DANVILLE SHORT LINE.
QUICKEST ROUTE TO
Norfolk, Old Pt. Comfort, and Virginia Beach.

TRAINS LEAVE EASTWARD.

Dist. Miles	STATIONS.	No. 2. Daily.	No. 4. Daily, except Sundays.	No. 6. Daily, except Sundays.
0	Leave Danville	8.10 a.m.		2.45 p.m.
7	Blanche	8.29		3.10
14	Milton	8.45		3.29
21	Semora	8.58		3.49
25	Cuningham	9.10		4.02
31	Alton	9.22		4.19
33	Harmony	9.30		4.26
35	Denniston Junction	9.35		4.31
38	Mayo	9.50		4.41
46	Virgilina	10.12		5.03
56	Atkins	10.40		5.29
62	Clarksville	10.52		5.41
64	Jeffress	11.08		5.50
67	Finchley	11.19		5.58
74	Boydton	11.40		6.14
77	Gills	11.43		6.17
81	Baskerville	11.59		6.30
85	Union Level	12.07 p.m.		6.38
91	South Hill	12.26		6.51
94	La Crosse	12.29		6.59
98	Brodnax	12.43		7.13
111	Lawrenceville	1.16	6.15 a.m.	7.45
116	Edgerton	1.45	6.30	
122	Pleasant Shade	2.04	6.48	
126	Durand	2.13	6.57	
130	Belfield	2.24	7.08	
134	James River Junction	2.34	7.18	
135	Green Plains	2.37	7.21	
139	Adams' Grove	2.42	7.26	
143	Drewryville	2.54	7.37	
149	Capron	3.12	7.52	
151	Pope	3.19	7.57	
157	Courtland	3.33	8.10	
160	Storys	3.37	8.17	
163	Isaacs	3.43	8.22	
165	Franklin	3.53	8.38	
167	Lee's Mill	3.58	8.33	
171	Elwood	4.08	8.41	
174	Holland	4.14	8.48	
176	Daughtrey	4.19	8.53	
178	Copeland	4.27	8.58	
181	Manning	4.32	9.04	
185	Suffolk	4.42	9.14	
189	Lindale	4.52	9.23	
191	Beamon	4.57	9.28	
194	Shoulder's Hill	5.04	9.34	
196	Peake's Siding	5.08	9.39	
199	Hodge's Ferry	5.13	9.46	
200	Bunting	5.17	9.49	
202	Duncan	5.21	9.55	
205	Arrive Portsmouth	5.30	10.00	
	Arrive Norfolk	5.50 p.m.	10.20 a.m.	

BAY LINE STEAMERS.
Leave Portsmouth 5.50 P. M.   Arrive Old Point Comfort 7.20 P. M.,
Baltimore 7.00 A. M.

NEW YORK, PHILADELPHIA & NORFOLK R. R.
Leave Portsmouth 5.55 P. M.   Arrive Old Point Comfort 7.20 P. M.,
Baltimore 6.45 A. M., Philadelphia 5.10 A. M., New York 8.00 A. M.

Pullman Sleeping Cars Cape Charles to Philadelphia and New York without change.

In this May 11, 1891 schedule, the A&D advertised itself as the "Danville Short Line" between Old Point Comfort, Norfolk, Portsmouth, Buffalo Lithia Springs, Danville and Points South. In addition to the daily through service between Norfolk and Danville, daily except Sunday service was also offered between Norfolk and Lawrenceville and between Lawrenceville and Danville. At that time, three trains were also being operated in each direction daily except Sunday over the West Norfolk branch; two trains daily except Sunday in each direction over the Claremont Branch; and, two trains daily except Sunday in each direction between Buffalo Junction and the Springs. (William E. Griffin, Jr. Collection)

the rolling stock that they had furnished to the A&D.

In November, 1891, Charles Cromwell resigned and the A&D continued to operate under the direction of Alfred P. Thom as the sole receiver of the property. The A&D's principal offices were retained in Portsmouth and at the 1892 stockholders' meeting, Benjamin Newgass was elected President and a member of the company's board of directors. To effect economies, the Beamon branch was abandoned and a number of stations were closed on the James River Division.

On June 13, 1893, the Circuit Court issued a decree adjudging the rank of the liens against the A&D and, on November 20th, a decree was entered to foreclose the mortgage and order a judicial sale by special commissioners of all of the company's property and franchises.

The year 1893 was also marred by tragedy as the A&D suffered the worst train wreck of its history. On August 16th, a passenger train derailed on a high trestle near Milton, North Carolina and three passenger cars plunged into the ravine below. The Conductor and five passengers were killed; one Brakeman and seven passengers were injured.

Pursuant to the terms of the Circuit Court's decree, the A&D

was sold by special commissioners at a foreclosure sale on April 3, 1894. The company was purchased in the interest of the bondholders by Benjamin Newgass and O. H. Edinger for $1,105,000. The sale was confirmed by the court on April 26, 1894 and a decree of August 1, 1894 ordered conveyance to the purchasers.

Just prior to the delivery of the conveyance, the purchasers requested that the receiver take steps to abandon the A&D's terminal at Portsmouth. It had been determined that the A&D lacked sufficient traffic to support two deep water terminals and they believed that the West Norfolk facility was more desirable for the transaction of the railroad's business.

The receiver submitted the request to the court and, on June 16, 1894, the court entered an order that the receiver "... be, and is hereby, permitted to abandon the City of Portsmouth as the terminus of the Atlantic and Danville Railway Company, and the use of the street leading to the terminus in said city, and so much of the route between Shoulders Hill and Portsmouth as he may think advisable". Under authority of the order, the A&D abandoned the City of Portsmouth on June 27, 1894 and promptly removed all its tracks, office, depot, shops and roundhouse from the city.

The city was not happy with the A&D's decision to abandon its facilities in Portsmouth. Its citizens reasoned that the new company's action had caused Portsmouth to lose the consideration for which it had issued bonds and subscribed to stock to finance the construction of the railroad to the city.

The city filed suit against the railroad, but to no avail. The A&D prevailed in court. The Portsmouth line was thereafter operated as a branch to Shoulders Hill until December of 1933, when train service was suspended. Finally, the Portsmouth branch would be abandoned in 1939 except for a 1.8 mile segment from the Seaboard Air Line Railway crossing easterly to the Portsmouth waterfront north of the Navy Yard, which was sold to the Norfolk and Portsmouth Belt Line Railroad.

After Newgass had acquired the properties of the A&D in the foreclosure sale, the next step was to consummate a reorganization plan. At that time, the general corporation reorganization laws of Virginia provided that, in the case of such a foreclosure sale of all of the works and property of a company, the old company would be dissolved upon conveyance to the purchaser. Also, the corporation created by the sale would succeed to all franchises, rights and privileges of the first company. Hence, when Newgass and Edinger purchased the A&D by foreclosure, they adopted in the deed the corporate name of the old company and this conveyance also constituted a charter for a new corporation under the provisions of

A typical 1890's era A&D passenger train steams over one of the railroad's trestles at an unknown location. Probably taken on the eastern end of the line, the photograph was taken by a Norfolk photographer. (Mallory Hope Ferrell Collection)

the Virginia law. Thereafter, the new A&D corporation applied for and obtained a franchise from the State of North Carolina in an act ratified February 25, 1895.

Thus confirmed in the enjoyment of all the rights and franchises of the old company, the new corporation effected a reorganization by executing a new first mortgage to Mercantile Mortgage Company of New York dated January 1, 1895 to secure $1,500,000 of 5 percent bonds. The reorganization plan also provided for the sale of $3,200,000 preferred stock and $2,500,000 common stock.

Following the reorganization of the A&D, local influence returned to the company's Board of Directors. Other than the Englishmen, Benjamin Newgass (who continued to serve as President and Chairman of the Board) and one from New York, the other members came from communities along the A&D - two from Norfolk, three from Danville, one from Lawrenceville and one from Milton, North Carolina.

The A&D moved its principal office to Norfolk in 1895 and went about the business of rehabilitating the company. With its debt finally under control the company's finances began to improve.

In the 1897 annual report to the stockholders, President Newgass reported: "The financial condition of the Road is satisfactory ... The Company continues to conduct its business on a cash basis, and has no obligations beyond those of an ordinary character." The A&D's control over its expenditures was evidenced by the respectable operating ratio of 74 percent that was achieved in 1896-97. The operating ratio was even better - 71 percent - for the following year.

In 1897, the A&D declared a dividend - its first - of one percent of the preferred stock. Another dividend of one percent on the preferred stock was declared in 1898.

In both years, President Newgass informed the stockholders that the financial condition of the company was sufficient to pay a larger dividend, but ".... regard to the future interests of the Road has dictated to your directors the policy of further strengthening the cash reserves, with the view, when opportunities present themselves, for the building of branches, extensions, or for co-operating with others in doing so ..." Two such opportunities soon presented themselves to the A&D.

In 1898, President Newgass advised the stockholders that the A&D would take a proportionate interest with other trunk line railroads in the construction of a belt line railroad running between Portsmouth and Norfolk. The railroads had recognized that the weakness of the Norfolk railway network was that while all the lines were centered on the Elizabeth River, some were located on the left bank, others on the right, and in most cases they were without convenient connections. This resulted in delays and additional expense in the interchange of freight between the lines. To establish direct connections between the various railroads, a belt line (known as the Norfolk and Portsmouth Belt Line Railroad) was built from Port Norfolk to the southeast below Portsmouth.

The second "opportunity" involved the construction of a branch line to a promising copper mine in North Carolina. On February 22, 1899, the A&D obtained a charter from the State of North Carolina to construct a railroad to be known as the North and South Carolina Railroad Company. It was intended that this railroad be extended to Columbia, South Carolina and a charter to that effect was obtained from the South Carolina legislature on February 27, 1899. The A&D owned all of the capital stock of the North and South Carolina Railroad and paid all construction costs. Construction was begun on the A&D at Virgilina (named for its location on the Virginia/North Carolina border) and was extended southward for 3.75 miles through the North Carolina counties of Granville and Person to the Holloway Mines. The branch was opened for operation to the copper mine in the autumn of 1899 but was never completed beyond that point.

In fact, before any operations commenced on the North and South Carolina Railroad, the control and possession of the properties of the A&D passed to the Southern Railway Company under a lease. Under this lease, the Southern acquired all of the A&D's stock in the North and South Carolina Railroad Company and thereafter operated it as a branch line.

The lease by the A&D of its entire railroad to the Southern Railway for a period of 50 years was approved at a general meeting at the stockholders held in Norfolk on August 31, 1899. The formal lease was executed by the two railroad companies that same day and possession of the A&D properties passed to the Southern on September 1, 1899.

This lease marked the end of the first period of independent operation of the Atlantic and Danville. During that period, the A&D had tried to establish itself as a part of a major east/west rail system. However, the company's financial difficulties prevented it from building west of Danville to connect with midwestern railroads. As a result, the A&D had lost its opportunity to play a major role in Virginia's developing rail system.

This 1890 map of the A&D and its connections shows the ambitions of its founders that the railroad would establish itself as a major east-west rail carrier. However, its financial difficulties would prohibit it from achieving that goal. (William E. Griffin, Jr. Collection)

CHAPTER 2

THE NORFOLK DIVISION -
OPERATIONS UNDER LEASE TO THE SOUTHERN RAILWAY
1899-1949

The Southern Railway Company was created by the reorganization, merger and consolidation of a group of railroad companies that were primarily situated in the Southeastern United States. The company was formally organized in 1894 for the purpose of acquiring the property of the Richmond and West Point Terminal Railway and Warehouse Company, a holding company that controlled a number of railroads, including the vast rail system of the recently bankrupt Richmond and Danville (R&D). This reorganization was managed by J. Pierpont Morgan of the New York investment house of Drexel, Morgan and Company. The resultant corporation would be a network of Southern railroads completely dominated by Northern bankers.

Through the Richmond Terminal reorganization committee the Southern Railway acquired the property of 16 railroad companies at its inception. The company immediately set out to expand its rail empire and acquired, by direct purchase or through reorganization, the property of 13 additional railroads. By 1895, it owned or operated a rail system of more than 4,500 miles in seven states. It had grown to over 6,000 miles by 1900.

However, with a rail system that sprawled all over the Southeastern United States, the Southern still lacked a satisfactory deep water outlet. The only such terminal was located at the head of the York River some 40 miles east of Richmond at West Point, Virginia. This port was reached via the tracks of the former Richmond and York River Railroad, which had been controlled by the Richmond and Danville.

The R&D would have preferred a terminal on the Elizabeth River at Norfolk. However, since the 1880's, both the Richmond and Danville and the Atlantic Coast Line (ACL) had honored an agreement not to build a rail line into the territory of the Seaboard and Roanoke Railroad (a predecessor of the Seaboard Air Line Railway) in exchange for Seaboard's commitment not to operate a

rail or steamship line into Richmond. One of the chief concerns of the new Southern Railway was how to achieve an entrance to the port of Norfolk without breaching the old R&D agreement with the Seaboard.

The Southern rationalized a way out of its dilemma. While it was bound by agreement not to construct its own line, the Southern reasoned that it would be free to use trackage built by some other company. The Southern saw an opportunity to establish itself on the Elizabeth River through acquisition of the Atlantic and Danville Railway.

In April of 1895, the Southern's President Samuel Spencer approached the new owners of the A&D with a proposal to purchase the line. In response to that proposal, A&D President Newgass wrote to Spencer that the pertinent point was " ... the price at which we would propose to dispose of the property". While not ruling out the sale of the A&D, Newgass cautioned Spencer not to "... treat the A&D as a bankrupt property, and it must be sold at that price. The road is a point or two above this". But Spencer was not obligated to pay Newgass' price to gain entry into Norfolk. He had an alternate plan and the Southern withdrew its bid to purchase the A&D.

Spencer brought the Southern into Norfolk in 1896 by leasing one North Carolina railroad and by obtaining track rights over two others. By a lease dated August 18, 1895, the North Carolina Railroad leased its entire line of railroad to the Southern for a period of 99 years beginning on January 1, 1896. Under this lease, the Southern obtained a line of railroad from Charlotte via Greensboro, to Goldsboro, North Carolina. On August 22, 1895, two predecessor companies of the Atlantic Coast Line Railroad Company executed substantially identical trackage rights agreements with the Southern. The Wilmington and Weldon granted to Southern the right to use its trackage between Selma and Tarboro, North Carolina. The Norfolk and Carolina Railroad granted to Southern the right to use its trackage between Tarboro and Pinners Point Junction, Virginia.

These trackage agreements extended the Southern's operations and route from Selma, North Carolina (a point on the North Carolina Railroad almost midway between Raleigh and Goldsboro) over the trackage of the Atlantic Coast Line into Pinners Point at Portsmouth, Virginia. Effective January 1, 1896, the Southern had established a route from Charlotte,

The Southern Railway maintained a fleet of 0-6-0 switchers at Pinners Point to handle switching assignments for the freight moving through the terminal via the A&D's Norfolk-Danville line and the North Carolina-ACL route via Selma, North Carolina. Southern A-7 class 0-6-0 No. 1626 is at Pinners Point on March 23, 1947. (H. Reid Photo)

Two locomotives that were operated over the Norfolk-Danville line are shown at the Pinners Point engine facility in 1949. To the right is Southern Ks class 2-8-0 No. 726 that was used on local freights between Pinners Point and Danville. To the left is Southern H-4 class 2-8-0 No. 390 that was used on the Suffolk-West Norfolk switcher. (L. D. Moore, Jr. Photo)

North Carolina to the Elizabeth River, serving Greensboro, Durham, Raleigh and Selma along the way.

The Southern promptly abandoned West Point as its principal deep water terminal and began to acquired property in Norfolk and at Pinners Point to built yards, wharves, docks and warehouses. The Southern, Atlantic Coast Line and Seaboard Air Line all established extensive terminals at Pinners Point, which is actually a peninsula lying between the western branch of the Elizabeth River and Scotts Creek. The Southern was now firmly established in Norfolk and within a few years the tonnage handled at Pinners Point was nearly three times as large as that formerly handled at West Point.

However, the Southern's situation at Norfolk was somewhat precarious. While the railroad had made substantial expenditures to build its Pinners Point terminal facilities, it was permanently dependent on the ACL trackage rights to reach them.

The Southern's management was given another reason to feel insecure about the situation at Norfolk when North Carolina Governor Daniel L. Russell attacked the lease of the North Carolina Railroad (NC RR). The State of North Carolina owned a majority of the NC RR's stock and Governor Russell's protest of the lease was a matter of patriotic state politics. He objected to the Southern's use of the NC RR to reach a Virginia port and the politics of his arguments made perfect sense to the citizens of North Carolina. In effect, a railroad owned by the State of North Carolina was being used to increase business handled through a port in Virginia rather than those in North

Carolina. The matter was hotly contested in the State legislature, but the Governor's recommendation to annul the lease was finally rejected. Nevertheless, this lease continued to be the subject of much ill-feeling and considerable litigation until finally upheld in the courts.

To protect its investment at Pinners Point from the whims of partisan North Carolina politics the Southern felt that it needed to acquire another route that would be separate and independent of the NC RR lease and the ACL trackage rights agreements. Consequently, the Southern resumed its efforts to acquire the A&D.

At the negotiating sessions between the two companies, the A&D was represented by Mr. Alfred P. Thom and the Southern by Mr. Fairfax Harrison. Thom was a Portsmouth attorney who had served as the A&D's court-appointed receiver and who was now employed as the railroad's General Counsel. Harrison, who had joined the Southern in 1896 at the age of twenty-seven, was a descendent of Lord Fairfax and several prominent Virginia families. Educated at Yale and Columbia universities in both law and finance, he was the assistant to Southern's President Samuel Spencer. Harrison would later serve as President of the Southern for twenty-five years (1913-37), far longer than any other chief executive in the railroad's history.

On May 11, 1899, the two railroads reached an agreement whereby the entire property of the A&D would be leased to the Southern for a period of 50 years. The agreement took effect on September 1, 1899 and would expire on July 1, 1949, with a provision giving Southern a right to renew for a further term of 99 years.

Southern agreed to maintain the property, pay all taxes, charges and assessments, and to pay an annual "fixed rental" and a cer-

Southern Ks class 2-8-0 No. 575 is ready for service at the Pinners Point terminal in 1949. This consolidation worked primarily on the Norfolk-Danville line during the period of the Southern lease and was one of the steam locomotives loaned to the A&D to protect local assignments until the new Alco diesels were delivered. (L. D. Moore, Jr. Photo)

Southern KS 2-8-0 No. 575 steams across the wooden trestle at Eastover heading towards Shoulders Hill and Suffolk on the West Norfolk line in 1948. (H. Reid Photo)

ain "contingent rental" for the use of the property. The annual fixed rental was based on a sliding scale which began at $127,000 per year for the first two years, increased progressively during the next ten years of the lease, and thereafter remained at $218,000 per year for the balance of the lease. The lease also provided for a contingent rental payable annually to the A&D equal to dividends on its common stock at whatever rate dividends were to be paid on Southern's common stock.

The A&D lease was certainly satisfactory to the railroad's British owners. Provision was made in the lease for a financial readjustment of the common and preferred stock issued by the A&D in its reorganization of 1894 as well as the refunding of the bonds issued under the first mortgage of January 1, 1895. The purpose of the readjustment was to convert the old bonds and preferred stock into a more marketable and income producing security which would be met by the rental paid by the Southern. Hence, after the lease had gone into effect, an amendment of the A&D charter was procured by an act approved February 7, 1900 which provided that all or any part of the A&D's preferred stock might be retired and mortgage bonds issued as might be deemed desirable. Under this provision, the A&D executed a new first mortgage dated May 5, 1900 with Mercantile Trust Company of New York and bonds were appropriated by the terms of the mortgage so that there could never be erected a fixed charge in excess of the A&D's income under the lease.

The Southern's rental payments would be sufficient to pay the interest of the A&D's outstanding first mortgage bonds, and were also enough to yield a solid 4 percent investment on the more than $3,000,000 of outstanding preferred stock (which was convertible into mortgage bonds). Prior to the lease, the A&D's preferred stock had never paid a dividend of more than a precarious one percent. Under the contingent rental agreement provisions of the lease, A&D's common stockholders stood a reasonably good chance of receiving some dividend before 1949. The A&D was also relieved of maintaining its corporate organization. The Southern hired most of the former A&D employees and the A&D's equipment and rolling stock were absorbed into the Southern's fleet.

The A&D reserved certain warehouses and riparian rights in Danville and also preserved its corporate existence throughout the term of the lease. In the early years of the lease, the A&D maintained its corporate office in the 745 Law Building at the corner of Plume and Granby streets in downtown Norfolk. On August 14, 1937, the office was relocated to the National Bank of Commerce Building in Norfolk, where it remained for the balance of the term of the lease.

The lease was also advantageous to the Southern. In addition to the revenues received after payment of the rentals and dividends, the Southern gained another entrance to the important terminal of Norfolk over trackage rights that it controlled. Even more importantly, the lease of the A&D freed the Southern from an absolute dependency on the use of the ACL trackage to reach the Norfolk harbor. Finally, control of the A&D protected the Southern in its lease of the North Carolina Railroad. With the A&D, the Southern established a route between Charlotte, North Carolina and Norfolk, Virginia that was independent of North Carolina Railroad and ACL trackage rights agreements.

However, the NC RR/ACL RR route via Selma, North Carolina would continue to be the Southern's preferred route into Norfolk because of the A&D's numerous grades (caused by the hasty and cheap construction techniques employed on the western end of the railroad), light rail and poor tie conditions. Writing to President Spencer on September 14, 1899 after an inventory of the property, Southern's General Manager F. S. Gannon reported that the A&D was " ... on the whole, the poorest roadway we have taken in this year ..." The other railroads acquired by the Southern in 1899 were the Atlantic and Yadkin Railway and the Northern Alabama Railway.

When the Southern took over the A&D on September 1, 1899, it began operations on a single track standard gauge railroad with over 200 miles of main line between West Norfolk and Danville. At that time, the A&D was also operating four branch lines (the standard gauge Portsmouth, Hitchcock, Buffalo Springs lines and the narrow gauge James River Division), and the branch between Virgilina and the Holloway Copper mine was under construction. During the lease, Southern operated trains on the A&D over that portion of the Richmond and Mecklenburg Railroad's line between Jeffress and Clarksville Junction under Southern's 1898 lease of the Richmond and Mecklenburg, no payments being required for such use.

The main line of the A&D was divided into two operating divisions: the Eastern Division extended from West Norfolk to Lawrenceville and the Western Division from Lawrenceville to Dan-

ville. On the Eastern Division, grades were moderate and the line passed through flat or gently rolling country. Sections of straight track prevailed, some of them several miles long. On the Western Division, curves were predominant along with short, broken or irregular grades of up to 1.5 percent.

Main line track was laid with 56-pound steel rail and rail ends were fastened together with fish plates rather than angle bars. There were no tie plates.

The crossties on the main line were practically all of hewn white oak. However, in the original construction of the line the crews had laid track with only 13 or 14 ties per rail. This was far short of the desired complement of 2,600 ties per mile.

Nor was there ballast anywhere on the railroad. The tracks were laid on clay west of Emporia and on sand from Emporia to West Norfolk. In rainy weather these tracks provided a rough ride.

Passenger trains in 1899 operated over this track in fair weather at 30 miles per hour, but not much faster. The steam locomotives were all coal burners and could pull a train of about fifteen cars. Only the locomotives had air brakes. The cars had no air brakes and most had link and pin couplers.

At the inception of the lease the A&D provided the Southern with 26 steam locomotives (23 standard, 3 narrow gauge) and over 800 cars. Only 21 of those cars were passenger coaches and most of the 720 freight cars were either box cars or flat cars.

About 78 percent of the A&D's carloadings in 1899 were derived from the transportation of lumber and cordwood. Local shipments of leaf tobacco accounted for another 3 percent with the remaining carloads derived from shipments of cotton, peanuts, copper ore, cattle, farm goods and local merchandise. Passenger revenue, including mail and express, accounted for about 25 percent of the A&D's earnings. Practically all of the revenue from passenger service was derived from local business.

The western terminal at Danville was adjacent to the Dan River. The Southern tracks at Danville crossed the A&D yard on a bridge about midway its length. The A&D yard consisted of tracks which were cut up into short sidings and spurs into private warehouses and team tracks. Structures included a 56-foot turntable, a wooden 2-track enginehouse, a water tank, a sandhouse and a combination freight and passenger station.

All of the stations along the line of road were painted frame buildings. Water tanks with a capacity of 25,000 to 30,000 gallons, were located a more or less 16-mile intervals. Two coaling stations were located on the main line, one at Angelica and another at Buffalo Junction.

The A&D's only repair shops were located at Lawrenceville

In a splendid view looking up at the train, H. Reid captured Southern Ks class 2-8-0 No. 575 handling another Suffolk-West Norfolk switcher assignment at Eastover on May 14, 1949. (H. Reid Photo)

about midway between West Norfolk and Danville. They had been built in 1895 and were in excellent condition when turned over to the Southern.

Although there were no long wooden bridges on the A&D main line, wooden trestles abounded. Most were of bent frame construction, but a few were pile trestles. Interestingly, the A&D's one truss bridge was located on the 8-mile Hitchcock Branch, which had been built to handle the lumber shipments to and from the Hitchcock Mill. The truss, 135-feet long and made of iron, had originally been built for, and erected on, the Shenandoah Valley Railroad in 1882. It was purchased by the A&D to span the Meherrin River on the branch in 1895.

West Norfolk was the eastern terminal of the A&D, where there were two small yards separated from the other by a highway crossing. The west yard contained three sidings, each about 2,000 feet long. The east yard was comprised of sidings, piers and buildings. Also at West Norfolk was a car shed, a water tank, a track scale, another 56-foot turntable, a 6-stall roundhouse, a house for employees, a depot, one transfer bridge and 4 piers.

But the Southern preferred to use its own terminal and piers at Pinners Point. There the Southern had concentrated all traffic moving to, from and through the port of Norfolk. Pinners Point was also where Southern connected with the Norfolk and Portsmouth Belt Line Railroad, which directly served most of the industries in the Norfolk/Portsmouth area.

After beginning operations under the lease, Southern abandoned the A&D's terminal facilities at West Norfolk and routed all traffic through the Pinners Point terminal. To reach Pinners Point from the A&D, Southern obtained trackage rights over the ACL from Boone to Pinners Point Junction, a distance of about 7 miles. Throughout the period of the Southern's lease, the A&D's trackage from West Norfolk to Boone was operated as a branch line.

After folding the A&D into its system, the Southern established a new operating division with headquarters at Norfolk. Designated the Norfolk Division, Lines East, this division was responsible for all operations over the old A&D and for all Southern trains operating over the ACL trackage between Pinners Point and Selma.

In 1930 the Norfolk Division was made a part of the Richmond Division, Lines East, which was headquartered in its namesake city, and comprised the Southern lines from Richmond to Danville and West Point. The A&D was operated as a part of the Richmond Division until termination of the Southern lease in 1949.

Of the 23 standard gauge steam locomotives renumbered and absorbed into the Southern system, all but two were 4-4-0 American type engines. No. 16 (renumbered Southern Railway No. 1313) was an 0-4-0 switcher. No. 26 (renumbered Southern Railway No. 1099), the lone 2-6-0 on the A&D roster, was destroyed when its boiler exploded at Franklin, Virginia

on January 11, 1904. The majority of the 4-4-0's remained on the A&D line until they were retired. All but one of these locomotives had been retired and scrapped by 1923.

The retirement of these locomotives and other pieces of A&D rolling stock resulted in a controversy between the A&D and the Southern as to the lessor's obligation under the lease for restitution of the A&D's original equipment. It was the A&D's position that Southern was obligated by the lease to not only make a unit for unit replacement of the retired A&D equipment but also to maintain equality in value, kind and condition. Southern disclaimed any such obligation and argued that its obligation under the lease was for mere equality of total value.

This dispute ultimately resulted in the institution of litigation by the A&D against the Southern. The matter was finally resolved in 1917 with an agreement between the two companies. This supplemental agreement to the original lease provided for an annual substitution by Southern of its equipment for the A&D equipment retired during each year. As of June 30th of each year, Southern furnished the A&D with a schedule showing the rolling stock and equipment retired during the year and the rolling stock and equipment as of that date which it proposed as substitutions. The A&D management was then required to approve the proposed substitutions. The supplemental agreement remained in effect for the duration of the lease.

For more than 30 years, Southern passenger trains operating over the A&D were powered by the 4-4-0 type locomotives and Southern's F-Class 4-6-0's. These tenwheelers were also assigned to mixed trains. Class E freight type 4-6-0's and Class H and J series 2-8-0's with 21" X 28" cylinders were assigned to handle the freight trains.

In 1932, Southern strengthened eight bridges on the A&D to permit operation of the 214,000 pound Consolidation type freight locomotives. Inasmuch as these Consolidations were permitted to operate double-headed without speed restrictions (and could handle all of the tonnage routed over the A&D line), the Southern found no justification for strengthening the A&D bridges for the operation of Mikado type locomotives. Hence, the K and Ks Class 2-8-0's were the heaviest steam freight locomotives to operate over the A&D.

Leaving Boone Tower in the distance, Southern Ks class 2-8-0 No. 723 is on ACL tracks in 1948 with a short eastbound freight enroute to Pinners Point. (H. Reid Photo)

13

Southern Ks class 2-8-0 No. 739 was another steam locomotive that worked primarily on the Norfolk-Danville line during the period of the lease. Here it steams by with a fine train of boxcar traffic on June 11, 1949. H. Reid captured the action on the section of the West Norfolk line between Eastover and Boone. (H. Reid Photo)

By the 1930's, most of the passenger runs were assigned to light Pacifics of the Ps, Ps-1 and Ps-2 Class. After 1926, all of these 4-6-2's were painted in the distinctive green and gold paint scheme fostered by Southern's President Fairfax Harrison.

During the early years of the lease, Southern scheduled two daily through passenger trains each way between Norfolk and Danville, a daily-except-Sunday local between Lawrenceville and Danville, and several branch line mixed trains. Train Nos. 1 and 2 departed in the early morning for their 7-hour daily Norfolk-Danville runs until finally discontinued in 1940. Trains Nos. 3 and 4 operated daily between Norfolk and Danville on a night schedule. They offered Pullman drawing-room sleeping car service between Norfolk and Charlotte, North Carolina, connecting with Southern's main line trains at Danville. Passengers to and from Norfolk were boarded and detrained at the Pinners Point depot with ferry service across the Elizabeth River to the Southern's wharf in Norfolk at the foot of Jackson Street. In the final years of passenger service, buses provided the transportation between Pinners Point and Norfolk.

With the exception of the Pullman service, Southern did little to provide for the comfort of its passengers. Only towards the end, when passenger traffic had nearly reached the vanishing point, did the Southern put on an air-conditioned coach. In fact, it was said that a journey over the A&D on a summer afternoon was an adventure to be contemplated with misgivings the one redeeming feature being the ride on the ferry boat "Memphis" or "Louisville" from Pinners Point to the company's wharf in Norfolk.

Train No. 5 was a daily-except-Sunday local that operated from Lawrenceville to Danville in the morning. Counterpart No. 6 returned in the evening. These trains were later operated as mixed trains until discontinued altogether in the 1930's. Mixed trains were also operated daily-except-Sunday on the Claremont Branch and between West Norfolk and Boone. In the gay nineties, A&D passenger trains made three round trips daily on the branch line between Buffalo Junction and resort at Buffalo Lithia Springs. It was a time when the resort was at the height of its popularity. By the time the Southern leased the A&D, patronage to the resort was on the wane, but mineral water continued to be bottled and shipped in great quantities from Buffalo Junction for many years.

When it came to handling freight traffic, the Selma line was the Southern's preferred route. The distance between Norfolk and Danville via the A&D's line was 206 miles, versus 317 miles by the Selma route. Between Norfolk and Greensboro, however, the A&D was only eleven miles shorter, an advantage thoroughly nullified by the Selma line's lower operating costs and transit time. It cost two or three times as much in wages and fuel to handle traffic over the A&D - and it took twice as long.

This was due to the fact that the Selma line was a physically better line than the A&D. During the period of the lease, the Southern improved the A&D by replacing 56-pound rail with 75-pound rail, installing tie plates, spreading ballast, renewing some trestles and eliminating others, and strengthening the bridges to support heavier motive power. Even with these improvements, however, the heaviest freight engines that could be operated over the A&D were the 100-ton 2-8-0's capable of pulling a train of only 1150 tons. Via the Selma line, 2-8-2's could handle 5,000 ton trains east of Selma; 2200 ton trains between Selma and Greensboro.

No wonder the Southern routed through freight between Danville and Pinners Point via Selma and not over the A&D. To the Southern, the value of the A&D lay in traffic originating and terminating at local points. The A&D was operated as just another Southern branch line. Freight service consisted of one local freight

Ks class 2-8-0 No. 739 was also one of the steam locomotives the Southern loaned to the A&D until all of its diesel locomotives had been received from Alco. In fact, the 739 has the distinction of being the last steam locomotive to operate on the A&D. It was retained at Pinners Point for emergency service until all of the startup problems were worked out with the new diesels and was not returned to the Southern until the fall of 1950. Here the 739 is shown switching freight by the water tank at the yard in Suffolk on June 11, 1949. (H. Reid Photo)

train in each direction, daily-except-Sunday, between Pinners Point and Lawrenceville, and between Lawrenceville and Danville. The typical freight transit time between Pinners Point and Danville was three days. The Southern also operated a switcher between Pinners Point, West Norfolk and Suffolk on week days.

Due to light freight traffic, service was suspended on all of the former A&D branch lines during the early Depression years and they were subsequently abandoned. The narrow gauge branch line between Emporia and Claremont was the first to be abandoned in 1932. Service was suspended on the Portsmouth Branch and on the North and South Carolina Railroad in 1933; the Hitchcock Branch in 1934; and, the Buffalo Springs Branch in 1935. The Southern finally received authority from the ICC to abandon and remove all of these branch lines in 1940.

By the early 1940's, the Southern had come to view its lease of the A&D as both unprofitable and unnecessary. Yearly deficits were incurred in the local operation and there was no thought of diverting the through traffic to the A&D because it was being handled more economically over the Selma line.

On March 27, 1944, the Southern formally advised the British owners of the A&D that it would not seek a renewal of the lease on July 1, 1949. However, there were obstacles to be overcome before the Southern could sever its relationship with the A&D.

At the time the Southern leased the A&D in 1899, there was no federal law regulating the construction, acquisition or abandonment of railroads. Had the law remained unchanged the property would have automatically reverted to the A&D's owners on July 1, 1949. However, by reason of changes in the law due to the Transportation Act of 1920, Southern could not cease operation of the A&D without first obtaining a certificate of public convenience and necessity from the Interstate Commerce Commission. This meant that Southern, if unable to secure the certificate to abandon the A&D, would be compelled to continue operation even though its contractual right to do so had ceased to exist.

The Southern also had to resolve a dispute with the A&D's owners concerning restoration of the A&D property upon termination of the lease. In 1899 the Southern had agreed to preserve, replace, renew and maintain the A&D in at least as good a condition, and as well provided for the carrying on of business, as at the time of original delivery and that the rolling stock and equipment would be returned in the same quantity, kind, value and condition of efficiency. Southern's unenviable task was to determine the 1949 equivalency of the railroad equipment and facilities that it received at the beginning of the lease in 1899.

Following the Southern's notice to A&D that it did not intend to renew the lease, informal conferences immediately began be-

Another Southern Ks class 2-8-0 used primarily on the Norfolk-Danville line was No. 757. This locomotive is shown switching the Union Bag Camp Paper Corporation yard at Franklin in 1948. To the left is the engine house of the Franklin and Carolina Railroad. (Mallory Hope Ferrell Photo)

Locomotive Engineer J. W. Browder, Sr. was at the throttle of 2-8-0 No. 757 when his son J. W. Browder, Jr. snapped this photo of his father switching hi[s] train at Lawrenceville. J. W. Browder, Jr. ("Wilbur Junior") would also become a locomotive engineer and worked for the Southern, A&D and NF&D. (J. W[.] Browder, Jr. Photo)

tween the representatives of the two railroads concerning the future of the A&D. At those conferences, the A&D's British owners were represented by a Norfolk attorney named Edward R. Baird, Jr. For many years, Baird's family had been associated with the A&D and in the years that followed he would spearhead the efforts to renew the independent operation of the railroad.

Baird's father had been elected to the A&D's Board of Directors in 1920 and later served as the company's Vice President and General Counsel. Edward Baird, Jr. was born in Norfolk in 1909 and graduated from the University of Virginia Law School in 1933. Following graduation, he joined his father's law firm and in 1934 - on his twenty-fifth birthday - he was elected to the A&D's Board of Directors.

From 1937 until 1941, the A&D maintained a one-room office next to Baird's law firm in the National Bank of Commerce Building in Norfolk. The A&D office was staffed by a secretary, Mrs. Charlotte Lee. When Mrs. Lee died in 1941, the separate office was closed and the A&D became practically another file in Baird's law office. From 1942 until 1946, Baird served as a naval legal officer. Upon his release from the Navy in 1946 Baird returned to Norfolk and became wholly consumed with the A&D's efforts to reorganize and resume independent operation.

In January, 1947, negotiations began between Baird, as counsel for the A&D, and officers of the Southern. The key issue was Southern's obligations under the restitution clause of the lease. Possible renewal of the lease at a lower rental was also discussed. These negotiations continued through the Spring of 1947.

In April, 1947, Baird notified the Southern that two protective committees had been formed and that they had insisted on participating in any further talks between the two railroads. One protective committee represented the A&D's first mortgage bondholders and the other represented its second mortgage bondholders. In May of 1947, representatives of these two committees joined representatives of the A&D in negotiations with the Southern.

On July 22, 1947, Southern notified Baird and the representatives of the two A&D protective committees that Southern had come to the conclusion that it did not desire to extend the lease of the A&D on any terms and that it proposed to turn back the leased property to the A&D at the termination of the lease in the condition required by the terms thereof. That same date, the Southern's

Board of Directors authorized application to the ICC for a certifi cate to abandon operation of the A&D.

At conferences held in August and September, 1947, Baird de manded that Southern restore or replace numerous A&D structure[s] and facilities, such as the rebuilding of piers and the terminal a[t] West Norfolk; restoration of the Lawrenceville shops; the renewa[l] of bridges; and, a unit-for-unit substitution to restore the origina[l] A&D inventory of over 800 units of rolling stock. On the othe[r] hand, Southern felt that its obligation was to restore the A&D a[s] a railroad as capable of handling its present traffic as was the rail road which Southern leased in 1899. The negotiations eventuall[y] broke down because of the considerable differences of opinion be tween the parties over the meaning of the lease.

Shortly thereafter, on November 26, 1947, Baird filed a suit o[n] behalf of the A&D against the Southern in the state circuit court o[f] Norfolk County, Virginia, seeking a declaratory judgment to estab lish Southern's restitution obligations under the lease. In addition the A&D asked for damages against Southern in the amount o[f] $4,000,000.

In March, 1948, a suit was brought in the federal district cour[t] in Richmond by the protective committee for the holders of A&D'[s] first mortgage bonds seeking $6,000,000 in damages for South ern's alleged failure to maintain the A&D's property in the manne[r] required by the lease.

The A&D won the opening round of its legal battle with South ern over the interpretation of the lease. In April, 1948, a hearing was held on the declaratory judgment suit and Judge Edward L[.] Oast entered an interlocutory decree favorable in part to the A&D[.] The judge then appointed a special commissioner to determine the exact extent of Southern's restoration obligations under the lease.

Southern appealed the decree and, pending a review by the Virginia Supreme Court of Appeals, resumed negotiations with the A&D and the two bondholder protective committees. Baird real ized that the A&D would have to do more than simply win its sui[t] against the Southern if it was to successfully resume independen[t] operations. In fact, the company's lack of an operating organiza tion led many to question whether the A&D would be able to oper ate its own railroad. The A&D was only a paper corporation with no financial resources and no actual railroad organization.

The physical condition of the A&D also presented significan[t]

problems. The A&D was actually comprised of two separate sections of railroad. Before it could operate through service between Norfolk and Danville, the A&D would have to obtain trackage rights from the Southern to bridge the 1.8 mile gap between the two sections of its line at Jeffress and Clarksville Junction. Also, on the western end of the line, the A&D had no terminal facilities at Danville and its only connection for the interchange of traffic would be with the Southern. On the eastern end of the line, the A&D had no terminal at West Norfolk and it would be required to obtain trackage rights over the ACL to reach Pinners Point where it could interchange traffic with other railroads. Obviously, the A&D had to find a way to amicably resolve its differences with the Southern.

Negotiations between the two railroads continued, and in May of 1948, a compromise settlement was reached. Under this settlement, the Southern agreed to pay the A&D $3,000,000 in cash in full settlement of all of Southern's obligations under the lease. The A&D property would be returned to it, when authorized by the ICC, in its present condition. This included the rolling stock owned by the A&D (other than locomotives and floating equipment) consisting of about 150 freight cars and 7 passenger cars.

Southern also agreed to permit the A&D to use, without charge, the 10 steam locomotives (3 light 4-6-2's and 7 Ks Class 2-8-0's) then being used on the A&D for as long as the A&D might desire.

To insure the continuity of A&D's line between West Norfolk and Danville, Southern agreed to grant trackage rights over the Richmond and Mecklenburg Railroad between Jeffress and Clarksville Junction. The A&D would be required to pay its user proportion of maintenance expenses and a fee which amounted to 4 percent of the valuation of that segment of track.

Southern agreed to act as a friendly connection of the A&D and to participate in numerous through routes and joint rates. If A&D desired, Southern also agreed to perform certain equipment maintenance work for the A&D and to give it the use of terminal facilities at Pinners Point and at Danville, at fixed rates for a term of three years.

Finally, Southern agreed to give the A&D an option to buy, at stated prices, approximately 190 units of rolling stock. It also agreed to construct at cost such shops, buildings and facilities as the A&D might decide that it needed and all of such items would be charged against the $3,000,000 cash settlement.

After this compromise settlement was reached, the owners of the A&D set out to transform the company from a paper corporation into an operating railroad. The first step was taken at a reorganization meeting of the Board of Directors held in Norfolk on August 26, 1948. At that meeting, the Board elected Earl L. Keister to be President, succeeding Edgar Newgass of England.

Most of the A&D's stock was still owned by the heirs of Benjamin Newgass. However, since the A&D would require active supervision under independent operation, the Newgass estate was willing to sell its stock to local interests so as to effect a "repatriation" of the railroad. The resignation of Edgar Newgass as President in favor Keister would help to pave the way for "home rule" (instead of "absentee" ownership) of the A&D.

The A&D was fortunate to obtain the services of Keister. His father had recently retired as General Manager-Central Lines of the Southern Railway System. Like his father, Keister had spend his entire railroad career with the Southern and had risen through the ranks to become, at age 45, the Superintendent of the Danville Division. In that position he had gained a knowledge of the A&D and with his background in both engineering and transportation, he was ideally suited to set up an operating organization for the new railroad.

His first order of business was to supervise the handling of two legal proceedings to separate the A&D from the Southern lease. First, final court approval of the compromise settlement had to be obtained. Next, the approval of the ICC was required before the Southern could abandon the line and the A&D take it over.

When a hearing on the settlement was set in the Circuit Court, the two bondholder protective committees intervened and joined in the A&D's request that the court enter an order approving the compromise settlement. Such a decree was entered on September 21, 1948 and the A&D's suit against the Southern was dismissed. In confirming the agreement reached by the two railroads, Judge Oast concluded his opinion as follows: "So that the Court had no choice but to approve a compromise which to me was apparently so advantageous to all parties concerned. It verged on the miraculous".

However, the whole compromise agreement was contingent upon the

Locomotive Engineer J. W. Browder, Sr. at the throttle of Ks class 2-8-0 No. 757 at Lawrenceville. Note that "Richmond" has been stenciled under the road number on the locomotive's cab. This indicates that the locomotive was assigned to the Southern Railway's Richmond Operating Division. After folding the A&D into its system in 1899, the Southern Railway created a new operating division with headquarters at Norfolk. Designated the Norfolk Division, its directed operations over the leased A&D line and Southern trains operating over ACL trackage rights between Pinners Point and Selma. In 1930, the Norfolk Division was made a part of the Richmond Division, Lines East that directed the operations over the Southern lines from Richmond to Danville and West Point. The leased A&D was operated as a part of the Richmond Division until the end of the lease in 1949. (J. W. Browder, Jr. Photo)

ICC's approval of Southern's application to abandon the operation of the railroad and the A&D's re-capitalization plan to modify its financial structure. On October 18, 1948, the ICC opened a public hearing on the application at the Monticello Hotel in Norfolk. Some 25 lawyers, representing the railroads, their employees, the bondholders, creditors and more than 100 civic and business interests, were present for the proceedings.

The case heard by the ICC examiners was unusual if not unique in the annuals of the Commission. Usually, abandonment proceedings were noted for the discordance of the diverse economic interests. However, in the A&D case there was a virtual unanimity among the lessor, lessee, security holders, shippers, employees and local communities that operation of the railroad should be discontinued by the Southern and resumed by the A&D.

The real issue to be decided by the ICC was whether the A&D would be able to render efficient and adequate service to the public under independent operation. If the ICC determined that the present and future public convenience and necessity did not permit the abandonment of the line by the Southern, then it could hold that Southern had a duty to continue the operation at a rental to be fixed by the Commission.

The examiners heard three days of testimony before closing the proceedings. As the year 1948 passed into history, the officers of the Southern and the A&D were still anxiously awaiting the ICC's decision.

Richmond Division Employee Timetable No. 19, in effect November 17, 1940.

18

In January of 1940 a significant snow storm swept across Virginia. To keep the passenger trains moving during the storm, extra locomotives were added to the trains. Here a locomotive called for extra passenger service exudes steam from every opening in front of the Lawrenceville shops during the frigid weather. (J. W. Browder, Jr. Photo)

In a classic photograph, Southern Railway Ks class 2-8-0 No. 682 stops at Boydton with a westbound local freight in 1949. (Flourney Photo/Virginia State Library)

Southern Railway Ks class 2-8-0 No. 682 with a westbound freight approaches Jeffress in 1949. (Flourney Photo/Virginia State Library)

Southern Railway steam locomotives operating from Danville to Norfolk over the A&D or from Danville to Richmond and West Point were serviced at the Dundee Yard engine facility at Danville. Here, KS class 2-8-0 No. 850 is shown with other steam locomotives at Dundee on October 27, 1946. (David Driscoll Photo/Tom E. Wicker Collection)

There was a crowd on hand to board the passenger train at South Hill. The date of the photograph is unknown but it was taken prior to 1924 when the Southern Railway built a new station at South Hill. The station in the photograph is the original station built at that location by the A&D. The photograph also predates much of the street and building construction that occurred around the train station at South Hill. (Josephine Shaw Collection/Courtesy the South Hill Railroad Museum)

This Southern Railway 1925-circa passenger train is approaching the South Hill station. While unidentified, the train is either No. 1 or No.2, the only passenger trains that were scheduled to arrive at South Hill in the daylight hours. The train has two coaches, a baggage car and a combination express/RPO car. The locomotive appears to be a B-10 class 4-4-0 American type engine. The Southern Railway never purchased a new American type engine from a builder, and this 4-4-0 is probably one that it inherited from the A&D when it leased the railroad in 1899. (Horace Clark Collection/Courtesy the South Hill Railroad Museum)

Beginning in the 1930's and until the end of the Southern's lease of the A&D, the passenger trains between Norfolk and Danville were assigned to light Pacifics of the Ps, Ps-1 and Ps-2 classes. After 1926 all of these beautiful steam locomotives were painted in the distinctive green and gold paint scheme fostered by the Southern Railway's president Fairfax Harrison. Southern Railway Ps class 4-6-2 No. 1234 is at Pinners Point in 1937. (Richard E. Prince Photo/C. K. Marsh, Jr. Collection)

The tugboat "Memphis" was used to tow barges and car floats between the two Southern Railway freight houses that were located on opposite banks of the Elizabeth River. It also ferried passengers between downtown Norfolk and the Southern's rail terminal at Pinners Point on the Portsmouth side of the river. Here we see the "Memphis" and Southern Railway Ps-2 class 4-6-2 No. 1353 with its passenger train at Pinners Point. (Mariner's Museum/Newport News, Virginia)

The shop forces at Pinners Point have Southern Railway Ps class 4-6-2 No. 1221 beautifully cleaned and ready for service in this 1937 photograph. The locomotive is at Pinners Point ready for its 8:50 a.m. departure with Train No. 1, with a 4:00 p.m. scheduled arrival in Danville. The passenger run from Pinners Point to Danville was 204 miles and was handled by engine crews without a crew change. Due to the mileage of the runs, engine crews in passenger service only had to work 20 days per month. (Richard E. Prince Photo/H. k. Vollrath Collection)

In a classic photograph, Ps class 4-6-2 No. 1227 pulls Train No. 1 away from Boydton in May of 1937 on its westbound run to Danville. Operating on a local schedule, No. 1 was scheduled to depart Boydton at 1:30 p.m. and arrived in Danville at 4:00 p.m. after making scheduled station stops at South Clarksville, Buffalo Junction, Virgilina, Denniston, Semora, Milton and Blanche. Tom Moore recalled that the arrival of Train No. 1 westbound was a town social event. Many of the townspeople would meet the train, socialize with their friends and then follow the mail truck up the hill to the post office where they picked up their mail. The mail truck was a Model T Ford roadster. (Thomas G. Moore Photo)

Southern Railway Train No. 4 is on ACL tracks at Armistead, between Boone and Pinners Point. The train will soon be making its 7:57 a. m. scheduled arrival at Pinners Point after making the overnight run from Danville. The locomotive is Southern Railway Ps-2 class 4-6-2 No. 1344 and the train has No. 4's typical consist of baggage car, express car, drawing room sleeping car and coach. The photograph was taken on June 21, 1949, a month prior to the end of the passenger service between Norfolk and Danville. (H. Reid Photo)

Beautiful Ps class 4-6-2 No. 1226 had the distinction of pulling the last passenger train from Pinners Point to Danville on the evening of July 31, 1949. The locomotive is shown here at Danville on August 25, 1933. (Bob's Photo)

At 7:27 p.m. on July 31, 1949, Southern Railway passenger train No. 3 departed Portsmouth for the night run to Danville. It was the last passenger train to ever operate over the A&D tracks. Pulling the train was Ps class 4-6-2 No. 1226, shown here arriving the N&W passenger station at Suffolk on its last run. (H. Reid Photo)

TABLE 1A — NORFOLK - PORTSMOUTH AND DANVILLE (Richmond Division)

Read Down 3	Miles	(ET) Eastern Time	Read Up 4
a 7 00 P.M.	....	Lv Norfolk ....Va. Ar	a 8 30 A.M.
a 7 27	.0	Portsmouth.......... "	a 7 57
7 45	6.1	Boone.......... "	7 40
8 13	17.4	Suffolk.......... "	7 13
f 8 28	25.1	Lummis.......... "	f 7 01
8 37	29.4	Holland.......... "	6 55
8 53	37.6	Franklin.......... "	6 42
9 13	46.1	Courtland.......... "	6 25
f 9 23	51.6	Pope.......... "	f 6 15
9 27	53.6	Capron.......... "	6 11
9 40	59.9	Drewryville.......... "	6 01
10 08	73.6	Emporia.......... "	5 40
f10 17	77.5	Durand.......... "	f 5 25
f10 29	83.9	Freeman.......... "	f 5 15
f10 41	89.1	Edgerton.......... "	5 06
10 50	94.2	Ar Lawrenceville...... " Lv	4 50
11 00	94.2	Lv Lawrenceville...... " Ar	4 50
11 25	107.3	Brodnax.......... "	4 28
11 35	111.1	LaCrosse.......... "	4 20
11 45	114.0	South Hill.......... "	4 10
11 57	120.5	Union Level.......... "	3 55
f12 05	123.9	Baskerville.......... "	3 47
12 22	130.9	Boydton.......... "	3 32
f12 33	137.8	Finchley.......... "	f 3 20
12 38	140.5	Jeffress.......... "	3 14
12 57	143.3	South Clarksville.... "	2 56
1 08	147.6	Buffalo Jct.......... "	f 2 43
f 1 18	153.1	Nelson.......... "	f 2 33
1 29	158.0	Virgilina.......... "	2 24
f 1 48	165.5	Mayo.......... "	f 2 08
f 2 27	184.5	Semora.......... "	1 35
f 2 40	191.2	Milton.......... "	1 23
3 15	205.2	Ar Danville.......... " Lv	1 00

Left margin: Last trip Train No. 3 from Norfolk July 31.

Right margin: Last trip Train No. 4 from Danville July 31.

Nos. 3 and 4, Drawing-room Sleeping Car (#) Norfolk-Portsmouth-Charlotte, (in Nos. 29 and 30 south of Danville). Shoulders Hill, Manning, Elwood, Isaac, Story, Arringdale, Adam Grove, Green Plain, Pleasant Shade, Antlers, Averett, Christie, Denniston, Alton, Cunningham and Blanche, flag stops for Nos. 3 and 4. f-Flag stop.
a—Via connecting bus between Southern Railway Station, foot of Jackson St., Norfolk, Va., and Southern Railway Broad Street Station, Portsmouth, Va.
#—Last trip from Charlotte July 30 and from Norfolk July 31.

The Southern Railway's public timetable of July 31, 1949 announced the last trips of Train Nos. 3 and 4 - and the end of passenger service between Norfolk and Danville.

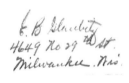

JULY 31st, 1949
LAST DAY OF OPERATION
DANVILLE & NORFOLK LINE
of the
Southern Railway System
After today freight service will continue under the name of the
Atlantic & Danville Railway

(Right) This envelope and RPO cancellation for Train No. 3 commemorate the last passenger run over the A&D. (William E. Griffin, Jr. Collection)

As passengers board Train No. 3's coach at Suffolk for the last run over the A&D, the Pullman Porter readies the Pullman car "McMullen" for sleeping car passengers. The Pullman crew of the "McMullen" on the last run were Conductor W. O. Compton and Porter G. R. Jones. (H. Reid Photo)

23

Pullman Porter G. R. Jones poses on the platform of the Suffolk station prior to the departure of Train No. 3 on its last run. The third man to the right of Porter Jones and facing right is Pullman Conductor W. O. Compton. (H. Reid Photo)

The engine crew of the last Southern Railway passenger train to operate over the A&D pose aboard Ps class 4-6-2 No. 1226. Seated is Locomotive Fireman J. C. Simmons. Standing is Locomotive Engineer E. H. Hudson. (Jacqueline Hudson Wheeler Collection)

The entire Southern Railway crew of No. 3 pose with Ps class 4-6-2 No. 1226 prior to making the last run from Portsmouth to Danville on July 31, 1949. From left to right they are: Baggagemaster O. C. Settle, Locomotive Engineer E. H. Hudson, Locomotive Fireman J. C. Simmons, Flagman A. J. Yarborough and Conductor T. P. Seymour. (Jacqueline Hudson Wheeler Collection)

CHAPTER 3

REBIRTH OF THE A&D -
INDEPENDENT OPERATION
1949-1962

The Southern Railway assisted the A&D when it returned to independent operation by adding six additional locomotives to its order for a group of 1500-horsepower RS-2 class diesel-electric road switchers that had been placed with the American Locomotive Company. However, as the date for the A&D takeover of operations approached, Alco advised that it would be unable to deliver the A&D diesels on schedule. Hence, the A&D would begin independent operations with two Alco RS-2's (Nos. 2105 and 2106) borrowed from the Southern Railway. No. 2105 is shown in this photo at Pinners Point on July 31, 1949, the day prior to the start of A&D independent operations, moving passenger equipment in position for the final passenger trips between Norfolk and Danville. (Eugene Hudson Photo/Jacqueline H. Wheeler Collection)

On March 30, 1949, the Interstate Commerce Commission issued its report. The Commission found that the Southern would be permitted to abandon operation of the A&D. However, it withheld issuance of an authorization certificate until certain conditions were met.

While the prescribed conditions were substantially the same as those assumed by Southern in its compromise settlement with the A&D, the Commission also ordered that operation of the railroad could not be abandoned unless and until the A&D acquired terminal facilities at Pinners Point and trackage rights to reach the Norfolk and Portsmouth Belt Line. The A&D had no terminal at West Norfolk and in order to reach another railroad's terminal at Pinners Point for interchange of through traffic and the Belt Line to serve the Norfolk-Portsmouth area, it would be necessary to use the Atlantic Coast Line's tracks from Boone to Pinners Point Junction. Without that connection the A&D could not be independently operated.

The A&D would also have to operate its trains over the Southern-controlled Richmond and Mecklenburg Railroad for 1.87 miles between Jeffress and Clarksville Junction. This was the only connection between the two segments of the A&D's line and the Commission made the A&D's acquisition of trackage rights over this section of railroad a condition precedent to the abandonment of operations by Southern.

The ICC also required the A&D to submit a plan for its approval that would alter or modify the new company's financial structure. Such a plan would have to provide for the retirement of a portion of the A&D's outstanding mortgage bonds in cash and the issuance of new 50-year bonds to the present holders of the securities.

Another major concern was whether the A&D would be required to provide passenger service. At that time, the Southern was operating one daily passenger train in each direction between Norfolk and Danville consisting of a Pullman sleeping car, day coach and baggage car. Pullman passengers usually numbered only six and the coach riders were typically local station-to-station fares. The new operators of the A&D were aware that the Southern had been losing money on this service and they feared that deficits from passenger trains might jeopardize the whole operation.

When the A&D petitioned the State Corporation Commission of Virginia to discontinue passenger service, the towns along the right of way offered only mild resistance. The State Corporation Commission, while granting that " ... it may well be that under normal railroad operating conditions, passenger service should be furnished ...", decided that "... the new operator should be given a chance to firmly establish itself with as little financial expense as may be possible".

The Commission authorized the A&D to discontinue passenger service for one year commencing with its independent operation of the railroad. However, service was never to be resumed and when Pacific No. 1226 pulled Train No. 3 out of Portsmouth at 7:27 p.m. on July 31, 1949, it went down in history as the last passenger train to ever operate over the A&D. The crew of that final passenger train was Engineer E. H. Hudson, Fireman J. C. Simmons, Conductor T. P. Seymour, Flagman A. J. Yardborough and Baggagemaster O. C. Settle.

The A&D had initially set July 1 as the date to resume independent operation. However, the ICC did not issue its final order until July 20. On that date, the Commission approved the application for abandonment of operation by Southern and for issuance of securities and acquisition of trackage rights by the A&D. It also approved an agreement reached by the A&D with the ACL for use of the Coast Line's yard and pier facilities at Pinners Point. Everything was now in place for the independent operation of the A&D to pass from the Southern to the independent company at midnight on July 31, 1949.

The A&D officials knew that it was not going to be easy - especially for a railroad that had not operated a train of its own in fifty years. And the A&D would be faced with direct competition

The A&D returned the Southern Railway diesels within a week. A&D RS-2 No. 101 was delivered on August 3 and No. 102 arrived on August 9. They immediately went into service handling A&D through freight service on Trains 85/86. When the first A&D diesel was placed in service employees and officials gathered for photographs with the new locomotive at West Norfolk. Standing on the ground to the far right in front of the 101 is West Norfolk agent Robert T. Rainey. The other employees, probably members of the train crew, are unidentified. (William E. Griffin, Jr. Collection)

from the Southern Railway for the business between Norfolk and Danville.

The new company did have a strategy for success. In addition to the existing local service, the A&D planned to establish a daily through freight service in each direction between the Norfolk area and Danville. This new overnight service would shorten the through freight time from two days to less than nine hours. No. 85, the daily westbound freight, would leave the ACL's Pinners Point yard at 10:01 p.m. and arrive at Danville at 6:40 a.m. the following morning. The daily eastbound freight, No. 86, would leave Danville at 8:45 p.m. and reach Pinners Point at 5:40 a.m.

To maintain that kind of schedule the A&D would need efficient and dependable motive power. President Keister decided to invest a portion of the cash received in the settlement with the Southern and replace the borrowed steam locomotives with a fleet of brand new diesels.

At that time, the Southern was purchasing a group of 1500-h.p. RS-2 diesel-electric road switchers from the American Locomotive Company. To assist the A&D, the Southern added six additional locomotives to one of its orders and the builder promised delivery in June of 1949.

However, as the date for the A&D takeover approached, Alco advised that the diesels could not be delivered on schedule. The A&D would have to begin independent operation with six 2-8-0 Consolidation type steam locomotives and two diesels borrowed from the Southern.

The first train to be operated by the new A&D was No. 69, the East End Local Freight, which departed Pinners Point for Lawrenceville with four loads and one empty at 6:20 a.m. on Monday, August 1, 1949. No. 69's motive power was 2-8-0 No. 575 with Engineer J. W. Browder, Sr. and Conductor J. A. McCutchen.

No. 69's eastbound counterpart, No. 70, departed Lawrenceville at 6:40 a.m. for Pinners Point behind 2-8-0 No. 739. No. 65, the tri-weekly West End Local, departed Lawrenceville at 7:10 a.m.

for Danville behind 2-8-0 No. 723. The 723 returned to Lawrenceville the following day with Train No. 66, the eastbound West End Local.

The A&D's new through freights made their first trips with borrowed Southern Railway diesels. Train No. 86 departed Danville at 9:00 p.m. on August 1st. behind Southern RS-2 No. 2105 with fourteen loads and ten empties. Train No. 85 departed Pinners Point at 10:30 p.m. behind Southern RS-2 No. 2106 with five loads and no empties.

Earlier that day, RS-2 No. 2106 had been used by the A&D to handle Local Freight Train 200/201. This was a turnaround local freight assignment that operated from Pinners Point to Suffolk and return daily except Sunday. The diesel that arrived on Train 86 at Pinners Point was used on Trains 200/201, then back to Danville

Posing in the cab of the 101 on August 9, 1949 are the two officials who were primarily responsible for the rebirth of the A&D. To the left is Earl L. Keister, the first president of the A&D after it returned to independent operation. To the right is Edward R. Baird, Jr., the Norfolk attorney who led the legal battle to return the A&D to independent operation. He would serve as the railroad's corporate secretary-treasurer. (William E. Griffin, Jr. Collection)

on Train 85 the same night.

The Southern diesels were returned within a week to Danville. A&D RS-2 No. 101 was delivered by Alco on August 3, 1949 and the 102 arrived on August 9th. They were promptly put into through freight service on Trains 86/85.

Southern Railway Consolidations 575, 584, 682, 723, 739 and 850 handled A&D local freight assignments until the remaining four diesels on order were delivered. RS-2's 103 and 104 arrived in October, 1949, with Nos. 105 and 106 delivered in November, 1949. Southern 2-8-0 No. 739 was the last steam locomotive to operate on the A&D. It was kept at Pinners Point for emergency use until returned to the Southern in October, 1950.

In addition to the new motive power, the A&D management knew that it would also have to improve track conditions to maintain the overnight through freight schedule. The nature of the Southern's local operation had required few improvements and by 1949 most of the A&D's main line rail had been in service for over forty years. Only 14 percent of the main line was laid with 80 to 85-pound rail. The rest of the railroad was laid with 70 to 75-pound rail and there was even some 60-pound rail on the line between West Norfolk and Boone.

The entire railroad was approximately 60 percent tie-plated, with 65 percent treated ties, but there was very little standard stone ballast. Most of the ballast was limestone screening and cinders, and much of that was either badly fouled or had disappeared into the subgrade.

The A&D proposed a rail replacement program that would involve laying 8 miles of new 80-pound rail each year. As the 75-pound rail was removed from the main line, it would be used to replace the much lighter rail on yard tracks and on the portion of the line between West Norfolk and Boone.

The A&D also proposed to start a tie plate installation program in 1950 to prolong the life of the ties. If revenues permitted tie plates would be installed on 25 miles of the line each year until the railroad was fully tie plated.

The western half of the railroad was to receive special attention. West of Lawrenceville, the line contained a number of grades, curves and bridges that necessitated a reduction in the speed of the trains. As the through traffic increased, it became a standard procedure to use two diesels on Trains 86/85. In addition to ordinary maintenance, the west end was going to require substantial improvements.

The new A&D operated neither shops nor terminal facilities of its own. At Pinners Point, the Atlantic Coast Line crews handled the switching duties and ACL shop forces serviced and made running repairs to the A&D diesels. The A&D's only car inspector was located at Lawrenceville.

Repairs and service to A&D rolling stock and locomotives were handled by the Southern under contract at Danville. A&D diesels that required heavy repairs, engine overhaul or wheel work were sent to the Southern's shop at Spencer, North Carolina.

Under the compromise agreement with Southern, the A&D was to receive the rolling stock then assigned and belonging to it. This consisted of 7 passenger train cars, 141 freight cars and 5 pieces of work equipment. However, Southern later agreed to let the A&D substitute other cars more adaptable to its operations in place of some of the cars to which it was entitled under the compromise settlement. Instead of taking the passenger cars, 62 flat cars and 9 log cars, the A&D selected wood rack cars and boxcars. As a result, the A&D commenced operation with 80 boxcars, 67 wood rack cars and 3 flat cars, for a total of 150 freight cars.

Hence, from the stand point of equipment and operations, the A&D began independent operation in a sound position. The energetic Earl Keister had done a remarkable job of setting up an operating organization for the new railroad.

The new A&D was headquartered in the three-story building at 115 West Tazewell Street in Norfolk that had formerly been occupied by the Virginian-Pilot newspaper and the Virginia State Employment Service. Off-line traffic agencies were established in New York, Atlanta, Birmingham and Washington, D.C. with division freight agencies in Norfolk and Danville.

For his management team, Keister brought W. H. Flowers with him from the Southern to serve as his assistant. L. Dean Curtis was recruited from the Belt Railway of Chicago to serve as Vice President and Traffic Manager. Another Southern Railway veteran, S. M. Percival, was hired as Chief Engineer-Superintendent. Edward R. Baird served as the Secretary-Treasurer and General Counsel. W. F. Bonney came from the Norfolk Southern to handle the duties of Comptroller and Industrial Agent.

The work force was largely recruited from the Southern Railway personnel and Keister was keenly aware that they might be a little skeptical about the prospects for the new A&D. Therefore, on the day before independent operations began, he staged an employee picnic at Lawrenceville as a get acquainted session. The event was so successful that it was repeated each year for the em-

Until the remaining four diesels ordered by the A&D arrived from Alco, the railroad operated its local freight assignments with steam locomotives borrowed from the Southern Railway. Ks-class 2-8-0's Nos. 575, 584, 682, 723, 739 and 850 had all operated on the A&D during the period of the Southern lease and they continued to handle A&D assignments until the last diesels arrived in November of 1949. This photo perfectly captures the transition of the A&D from the Southern Railway lease to independent operation. Southern Railway Ks-class 2-8-0 No. 682, with an A&D boxcar behind the locomotive, is shown crossing over a bridge that has been recently stenciled for the A&D Railway. (Virginia State Library)

Westbound							NORFOLK—LAWRENCEVILLE	Eastbound		
THIRD CLASS	FIRST CLASS		Capacity of Tracks in Cars		Miles from West Norfolk	Station Nos.	TIME TABLE NO. 1 — In effect August 1, 1949	FIRST CLASS	THIRD CLASS	THIRD CLASS
201 Ex. Sun.	69 Ex. Sun.	85 Daily	Siding	Other			STATIONS	86 Daily	70 Ex. Sun.	200 Ex. Sun.
A.M.	A.M.	P.M.					Lv. .... Ar.	A.M.	P.M.	P.M.
7.05	6.00[86]	10.01		Yard	13.1	B-236	WYCX.PINNERS POINT...N	5.40[69]	12.20	1.15
							7.1			
7.40	6.25	10.30		20	6.0	6	X.....BOONE.....N	5.10	11.55[200]	12.50 / 11.30[70]
							2.8			
7.46	6.31	10.36		50	8.8	9	SHOULDERS HILL	5.04	11.48	11.23
							3.2			
7.52	6.37	10.42		25	12.0	12	BEAMON	4.58	11.40	11.15
							5.3			
8.05		10.56		17.3	18	18	WX.....SUFFOLK.....D	4.44		11.01
							0.7			
A.M.	7.10	10.58	43	Yard	18.0		SUFFOLK SIDING	4.42	11.15	A.M.
							7.0			
	7.23	11.14		22	25.0	25	LUMMIS	4.26	10.55	
							4.3			
	7.31	11.23		82	29.3	29	X.....HOLLAND.....D	4.17	10.45	
							8.2			
	7.55	11.47	35	30	37.5	38	WX.....FRANKLIN.....D	3.53	10.25	
							5.4			
	8.05	11.59	45		42.9	43	STORY	3.41	9.55	
							3.1			
	8.15	12.07	35	16	46.0	46	X.....COURTLAND.....D	3.33	9.45	
							5.5			
	8.30	12.20		34	51.5	52	POPE	3.20	9.30	
							2.0			
	8.35	12.24		38	53.5	54	CAPRON.....D	3.16	9.25	
							2.4			
	8.45	12.30	35	15	55.9	56	WC.....ANGELICO	3.10	9.13	
							3.9			
	8.55	12.37		8	59.8	60	DREWRYVILLE	3.03	9.02	
							1.5			
	8.59[70]	12.41	41		61.3	61	ARRINGDALE	2.59	8.59[69]	
							3.4			
	9.15	12.47		8	64.7	65	ADAMS GROVE	2.53	8.40	
							3.3			
	9.30	12.55		16	68.5	68	GREEN PLAIN	2.45	8.25	
							5.0			
	10.20	1.05		Yard	73.5	73	WX.....EMPORIA.....N	2.35	8.10	
							7.6			
	10.40	1.20	44	2	81.1	81	PLEASANT SHADE	2.20	6.25	
							2.7			
	10.50	1.25		3	83.8	83	FREEMAN	2.15	6.20	
							5.2			
	11.01	1.39		26	89.0	89	EDGERTON	2.01	6.10	
							5.1			
A.M.	11.15 A.M.	1.50[86] A.M.	6	Yard	94.1	94	WTX.LAWRENCEVILLE...NC	1.50[85] A.M.	6.00 A.M.	A.M.
Ex. Sun. 201	Ex. Sun. 69	Daily 85					Ar. .... Lv.	Daily 86	Ex. Sun. 70	Ex. Sun. 200

struggling new railroad was provided with a welcome increase in traffic.

During this period, the construction of the huge Buggs Island hydroelectric dam (also known as the John H. Kerr Dam) on the Roanoke River near Clarksville, Virginia provided the company with quite a lucrative source of business. The project was served exclusively by the A&D and all materials and equipment in carload lots had to be routed over the A&D to Antlers, where connection was made with the U.S. Government's switching branch to the dam site.

The A&D experienced a steady increase in business. In January of 1951, the railroad handled 3,121 carloads - an increase of 1,393 over the previous January. For the year 1951, the A&D handled 35 percent more business than during the year 1950 and was moving twice the tonnage handled by the Southern during the period of the lease.

With respect to tonnage, about half of the increase occurred in construction and road building materials such as stone and sand for

This schedule from the A&D's Timetable No. 1, in effect August 1, 1949, shows the initial operations on the new A&D.

ployees and their families on the Sunday closest to the company's anniversary.

Keister and his aides also made frequent trips up and down the railroad, talking to employees and building pride in the A&D "family". To further develop a close knit organization, the railroad began to publish its own monthly magazine, The Chatterbox.

A strenuous public relations and traffic promotion campaign soon got underway and was followed by an industrial development program. Traffic Manager Curtis began speaking at civic clubs and organizations all along the line. Desk blotters and book matches were handed out and a series of full page advertisements were run each month in Traffic World, the shippers' magazine. These advertisements pointed out the opportunities for industrial development in Southside Virginia and stressed the improved freight service offered by the A&D. Curtis and Bonney also made frequent trips to encourage manufacturers to locate along the line. During the first year of operation they were successful in locating five new industries on the A&D.

However, for all of their efforts the revenues for the initial period of independent operation were disappointing. For its first five months the A&D showed a net railway operating loss of $73,482.

Business continued at a moderate rate during the first half of 1950 then accelerated in the last half of the year due to the outbreak of the Korean War. The A&D afforded rail connections to a number of military installations that became quite active as the rearmament proceeded. As the war stimulated traffic generally, the

Westbound							DANVILLE—LAWRENCEVILLE	Eastbound		
THIRD CLASS	SECOND CLASS	FIRST CLASS	Capacity of Tracks in Cars		Miles from West Norfolk	Station Nos.	TIME TABLE NO. 1 — In effect August 1, 1949	FIRST CLASS	THIRD CLASS	
65 Mon-Wed-Fri	Sou. Ry. Freight 67 Ex. Sun.	85 Daily	Siding	Other			STATIONS	86 Daily	Sou. Ry. Freight 68 Ex. Sun.	66 Tue-Thu-Sat.
A.M.	A.M.	A.M.					Lv. .... Ar.	A.M.	A.M.	A.M.
6.45		2.15[86]	6	Yard	94.1	94	WTX.LAWRENCEVILLE...NC	1.20[85]		12.00
							4.7			
7.00		2.26		22	98.8	99	CHARLIE HOPE	1.08		11.45
							8.4			
7.25		2.44	35	25	107.2	107	X.....BRODNAX.....D	12.52		11.25
							3.8			
7.35		2.52		22	111.0	111	X.....LA CROSSE.....D	12.44		11.15
							2.9			
8.00		2.59		60	113.9	114	WX.....SOUTH HILL.....D	12.37		11.00
							6.5			
8.16		3.12		20	120.4	120	UNION LEVEL	12.23		10.35
							3.4			
8.26		3.19		22	123.8	124	X.....BASKERVILLE.....D	12.15		10.25
							2.9			
8.35		3.27		8	126.7	127	ANTLERS	12.06		10.16
							4.1			
8.50		3.35	47	12	130.8	131	X.....BOYDTON.....D	11.57		10.05
							6.9			
9.07	A.M.	3.50		35	137.7	138	FINCHLEY	11.40	A.M.	9.45
							2.7			
9.40	7.25	3.58		60	140.4	140	X.....JEFFRESS	11.30	10.45	9.40
							2.0			
9.50	7.35	4.08			142.4		WC..CLARKSVILLE JCT.	11.20	10.35	9.17
							0.8			
9.55	A.M.	4.12		30	143.2	143	X.....SOUTH CLARKSVILLE.D	11.16	A.M.	9.14
							4.3			
10.07		4.23		12	147.5	147	X.....BUFFALO JUNCTION...D	11.04		9.00
							5.5			
10.17		4.36		24	153.0	153	NELSON	10.51		8.47
							4.0			
10.27		4.46		10	157.0	157	N. & S. C. JUNCTION	10.41		8.37
							0.9			
10.30		4.48	33	10	157.9	158	X.....VIRGILINA.....D	10.39		8.35
							3.8			
10.40		4.56		9	161.7	162	CHRISTIE	10.31		8.23
							3.7			
10.55		5.05		18	165.4	165	WX.....MAYO	10.22		8.17
							4.1			
11.05		5.15		25	169.5	169	X.....DENNISTON	10.12		8.02
							4.4			
11.17		5.26		12	173.9	174	ALTON	10.01		7.52
							5.6			
11.30		5.36		20	179.5	179	CUNNINGHAM	9.50		7.40
							4.9			
11.42		5.48		20	184.4	184	SEMORA	9.37		7.30
							6.7			
11.55		6.05		21	191.1	191	W.....MILTON	9.20		7.17
							5.9			
12.10		6.20		24	197.0	197	BLANCHE	9.05		7.05
							7.8			
12.25		6.35		Yard	204.8		X.....A. & D. YARD	8.50		6.50
							0.3			
12.30 P.M.	A.M.	6.40 A.M.		Yard	205.1	205	WYCX..DANVILLE	8.45 P.M.	A.M.	6.45 A.M.
Mon-Wed-Fri 65	Ex. Sun. 67	Daily 85					Ar. .... Lv.	Daily 86	Ex. Sun. 68	Tue-Thu-Sat. 66

The Schedule figures between Jeffress and Clarksville Jct. are for information only; the time tables, rules, and regulations of the Southern Railway will govern between these points.

MEASURE of PROGRESS

The beginning of our fourth year marks another step forward in the history of the A&D.... and it is a year measured in service for our many old friends as well new friends.

"For Service See...

No Matter How The Wind Blows...
You're SAFE Via A&D

BETTER SERVICE EVERYTIME

...AND BETTER SERVICE IS YOUR BUSINESS TOO!

"For Service See ..... The A&D"

ATLANTIC & DANVILLE RAILWAY
GENERAL OFFICES: 115 West Tazewell St., Norfolk 10, Va.

The independent A&D aggressively advertised its improved freight service.

the Buggs Island dam project. Healthy increases were also noted in a number of the diverse commodities that originated on the A&D such as: peanuts, industrial chemicals, tobacco, paper, pulpwood and fertilizer.

Because of the increased business, the A&D's Board of Directors authorized the purchase of another diesel locomotive. No. 107, a 1600-h.p. RS-3, was ordered from Alco in June and placed in service on July 1, 1951.

The A&D also utilized available funds to make a modest start in its program to improve the property. Five track miles of new 85-pound rail was laid in two different locations on the west end of the line: between Baskerville and Antlers, and between Christie and Mayo. It was the first new rail to have been laid on the A&D in 61 years, or since the line was completed in 1890.

Nearly four miles of relay 85-pound rail was also installed. Three miles of the relay rail was laid one and one-half miles west of South Hill and the balance was just east of Emporia.

During the year, 63,463 tie plates and 26,000 ties, the majority of which were treated, were also installed, along with 40,000 feet

of switch ties and 7,800 tons of crushed stone and screening ballast. The Hogan's Creek bridge was entirely renewed and work commenced on others.

However, the most significant event of 1951 was the sale by the British stockholders of their controlling interest in the A&D. In the reorganization hearings before the ICC the heirs of Benjamin Newgass had stated their intention to eventually sell their stock to local interests more directly concerned with the rail service who would also be in a position to influence the routing of traffic. The reorganization process had resulted in about 45 percent of the A&D's stock becoming American-owned.

In March, 1951, the British stockholders sold their 12,443 shares, approximately 55 percent of the total, to the six members of the A&D's Board of Directors. Subsequently, the Board members resold a substantial portion of the stock, without profit, to individuals or business interests in the territory served by the A&D. In this way, it was hoped that the A&D would have the unique advantage of being "home-owned" as well as "home-operated".

On the surface, the A&D appeared to be on its way to success. However, even in 1951, there were signs of serious trouble.

In fact, the A&D's gain in business was illusory. While the 35 percent increase in freight traffic had produced approximately 25 percent more revenue, transportation expenses alone had increased by approximately 40 percent. Maintenance and traffic expenses also advanced about 25 percent so that with other increased outlays and net results in 1951 were actually not as favorable as they had been in 1950. This change in the operating expenses spelled a change in the total operating ratio from 81.41 percent in 1950 to 85.54 percent in 1951. Such a ratio indicated that the company's expenses were abnormal.

Nearly every item of expense had substantially increased. Apart from the additional expense of simply handling more business, the A&D also had to contend with fixed joint facility rentals at Pinners Point and Danville, and the effect of inflation on the costs of fuel, supplies and wages - all items over which the A&D management had little or no control.

The expense for equipment hire was an item of special concern. The A&D owned very few cars that were suitable for class one loading and had to rely heavily on the use of foreign line cars for the traffic it generated on line. Since the rental expense for the use of these foreign cars (per diem) far exceeded the car hire earned by the A&D's antiquated fleet, the account for equipment hire would always fluctuate in proportion with the volume of business handled.

The A&D's maintenance program was another factor which offset the gain that might otherwise have been expected to follow from such a substantial increase in business. This program was closely geared to operations and the heavier the traffic, the greater would be the outlays on roadway.

In fact, the increased traffic was already beginning to take its toll on a roadway that had been neglected for so many years. During 1951, there were 44 percent more rail failures than in 1950.

The physical condition of the property was such that revenues from increased traffic would constantly have to be ploughed back into improvements and better facilities.

Traffic volume during the first half of 1952 continued to be impressive as carloads increased by 764 cars over the corresponding period for 1951. However, a national steel industry strike had a chilling effect on the economy and during the second half of the year carloadings decreased some 1,900 cars to create a deficit of approximately 1,200 cars for the year.

While gross revenues were up about $50,000 over 1951, they were less than anticipated and were accomplished by sizeable increases in both operating expenses and in equipment and facilities rentals. The operating ratio for 1952 showed a slight improvement but was still an unacceptable 85.17 percent.

Nevertheless, the A&D was able to continue with its maintenance program. During the year the railroad laid 3.79 miles of new 85-pound rail; installed 26,933 new crossties bringing the main line to 77 percent supplied with long-life ties; put on 74,476 tie plates bringing the main line to 70 percent tie-plated; and, unloaded 10,811 tons of stone and screening for ballast.

However, future improvements to the property would depend upon the company's financial position and during 1952 and 1953 the A&D suffered a series of significant setbacks.

On September 24, 1952, the ICC issued an order which required all freight cars used in interchange service to be equipped with AB-type brakes by January 1, 1953. None of the A&D's freight cars were equipped with AB brakes. Nor could the railroad

RS-2 No. 101 is at Suffolk with Train 200-201, the Suffolk-West Norfolk Switcher in 1953. To fully utilize its motive power, the A&D assigned the diesels that arrived on Train No. 86 to be used on Trains 200-201, then back to Danville on Train No. 85. (William B. Gwaltney Photo/C.K. Marsh, Jr. Collection)

afford to install them on its old rolling stock. To a railroad that was already spending too much for car hire, the ICC order was a staggering blow. After January 1, 1953 no A&D car could be loaded with shipments destined to points off line.

Two unfortunate derailments during the latter part of 1952 further aggravated the A&D's difficulties. Train No. 86, with diesel units 102 and 101, was traveling about 30 miles per hour with 42 loads and 5 empties when a rail broke under the train at Mile Post 51.25 near Pope, Virginia on October 19th, causing a derailment of 12 cars. Then, on December 12th, Local No. 65, diesel engine No. 106, handling 11 loads and 5 empties, derailed 8 cars when it rocked off the track while rounding the curve at Mile Post 109.8 near LaCrosse, Virginia. The derailment was caused by a defective center bearing on an ACL box car.

Outlays necessitated by the derailments were enough to affect the company's cash position. As a consequence, the A&D had to negotiate a demand loan of $100,000 in December with a local bank. This loan was repaid in large part out of a fund of $80,000 which the United States Government was obligated to pay the A&D account the relocation of its tracks at Clarksville due to the construction of the John H. Kerr Dam and Reservoir.

A series of events occurred in 1953 to adversely affect the A&D's earnings: hostilities ceased in Korea; the Kerr Dam and Reservoir were completed; a drought took place in the tobacco territory; and, there was less highway construction in Southside Virginia. The company suffered another serious setback during the year when the per diem rate was increased by 20 percent. Since the A&D relied heavily on foreign lines for freight cars, the increase in per diem rates further increased the A&D's already burdensome car hire expense.

Earnings during 1953 were insufficient for payment of contingent bond interest and the program of purchasing A&D mortgage bonds

In a terrific photograph of A&D operations, Train 201, the Suffolk-West Norfolk Switcher, is shown approaching Boone Tower behind RS-2 No. 104 on May 11, 1962. In a photo taken from the tower, the train is returning from West Norfolk and is enroute to Suffolk, crossing at grade the ACL's line from Pinners Point. To the right, note the connecting track between the ACL's Pinners Point-Rocky Mount line and the A&D's West Norfolk-Suffolk line. (Ralph Coleman Photo)

As Train 201 passes Boone Tower, the operator "hoops up" train orders to the A&D Conductor on caboose No. 109. Fortunately, Ralph Coleman was on hand to capture on film this moment of A&D train operation. (Ralph Coleman Photo)

on the market was virtually discontinued. Gearing expenditures to revenues, a reduction was made for the first time in the roadway maintenance program.

Subsequent to 1953, the A&D operated at substantial deficits in each year except 1956. The company was seriously affected by a post-war recession in business during 1954 and revenues showed a decrease of 15.97 percent. The deficit for the year amounted to $177,809. Thereafter, until 1962, the annual deficits ranged from $75,065 to $237,519.

Earl Keister resigned as the A&D's president effective April 1, 1954 to become president of the Tennessee Central Railway Company. Vice President L. D. Curtis was elected to succeed him and, in the interest of economy, the office of vice president was left vacant.

In an effort to reduce its net rents, the A&D began purchasing rebuilt boxcars in June of 1954. Twenty-five former New York Central steel 40-foot boxcars were purchased from the Ortner Company of Cincinnati, Ohio for $2,000 each on a five year conditional sales agreement. Numbered 2001 to 2025, they were the first cars to bear the distinctive A&D emblem with the road's name between two black concentric circles that were pierced by a blue arrow bearing the large letters "A&D".

However, even with the acquisition of additional used boxcars in 1955-56, freight car hire continued to be a serious problem for the A&D. Also, commencing in 1955 the A&D was required to pay out over $80,000 per year in fixed interest payments on its first and second mortgage bonds. The company's inability to generate enough revenue to meet these annual interest payments would be a major contributor to its financial difficulties. In December of 1955 the A&D was again required to negotiate

a loan from a local bank to provide operating funds.

As a result of the large and continuing deficits, funds were not available to properly maintain the property and equipment and by August of 1957, the A&D's motive power was badly in need of repair. Of seven units, four were out of service for repairs and the A&D was required to lease locomotives from other railroads just to operate its trains. The 102 was permanently removed from service in December of 1958.

Beginning in 1957, the company was required to negotiate loans each year to meet the interest payments on its bonds and to satisfy the outstanding debt on equipment and obligations.

Then, in 1958, the A&D defaulted on payments due the Southern Railway for use of trackage and the Danville terminal facilities. At the same time, the A&D was also unable to keep up payments to the ACL for the use of trackage and the Pinners Point terminal facilities. By July of 1959 the A&D was in arrears on payments to the ACL in excess of $150,000. The company's assets were also insufficient to settle its interline accounts with connecting carriers and, on September 29, 1959, the A&D suffered another major derailment that resulted in the destruction of several cars belonging to other railroads. The company could not even afford diesel fuel for its locomotives.

In desperation, the A&D made application in late 1959 to the ICC for a government guarantee of an $80,000 loan. The A&D made the loan application under the 1958 Transportation Act which had been passed to help railroads obtain needed financing under government guaranteed loans when they were unable to get money elsewhere.

On January 6, 1960, the ICC rejected the A&D's application. It was the first outright rejection of a loan application under the Transportation Act.

On January 19, 1960, the A&D petitioned the United States District Court for the Eastern District of Virginia at Norfolk for reorganization under Section 77 of the Bankruptcy Act. The railroad advised the court that it was unable to meet its debts as they ma-

The A&D's only RS-3 - the 107- departs Suffolk yard with a westbound freight train in 1961. The 1600-horsepower locomotive was added to the A&D's roster in 1951 as a result of the steady increase in business during its first year of operation. (William B. Gwaltney Photo/C. K. Marsh, Jr. Collection)

To compete for the traffic between Norfolk and Danville, the A&D's strategy was to establish a new daily overnight service (Trains 85/86) that would shorten the through freight transit time from two days to less than nine hours. On a slower schedule, the A&D also operated Trains 69/70 between Norfolk and Danville daily except Sunday. On March 10, 1959, eastbound Train No. 70, with RS-2 No. 101, meets its westbound counterpart No. 69, with RS-2 No. 103, at Franklin. (Mallory Hope Ferrell Photo)

tured. One of the first mortgage bondholders described the company as "hopelessly insolvent".

In February of 1960, Judge Walter E. Hoffman appointed Portsmouth businessman Seaborn J. Flournoy as sole trustee and directed him to continue operation of the railroad pending disposition of the bankruptcy proceeding.

However, the A&D's financial woes continued. In February the 101 was permanently retired and by the summer of 1960 only the 105 and 106 were still in service. To operate its trains, the A&D leased Alco S-2's from the Chesapeake and Ohio Railway and EMD GP-7's from the Seaboard Air Line Railway. The A&D did not have the money to repair its own locomotives.

In a hearing before the bankruptcy court, the trustee testified that he was unable to propose a plan for the continued independent operation of the railroad and recommended its sale as the only means of continuing a service required by the public. The A&D continued operations under direction of the trustee hoping for something that might change the economic outlook, such as the location of a large industry on its line. Nothing materialized and the railroad operated with deficits of $237,519 in 1960 and $75,061 in 1961.

In August of 1962, the trustee petitioned the court for authority to sell the railroad. He testified that the A&D would require over $1 million to put the rolling stock and trackage in a safe operating condition. According to Flournoy, there was not enough cash to continue operations and the railroad was in such condition that " ... one more wreck might destroy the equity that now remains".

On September 28, 1962, Judge Hoffman signed an order authorizing the sale. The A&D, 73 years old and ailing, would be sold to " ... the highest and best bidder".

The Norfolk and Western Railway was the only bidder. It bought the A&D for $1.5 million at a public auction held on the front steps of the Post Office Building in Norfolk, Virginia.

The achievements and high expectations of the early-1950's were now only bittersweet memories. Like many other short lines that failed during the post-war era, the A&D was simply unable to compete as an independent operator with the highway competition.

The last day the A&D operated was October 31, 1962. It is ironic that just as J. W. Browder, Sr. had been the engineer on the first train operated by the A&D, his son was an engineer on one of the last trains to operate. Mr. J. W. Browder, Jr. with Conductor V. V. Smith, Fireman H. M. Throckmorton, Brakeman O. B. Boyd and Flagman H. M. Panther were crew members of Extra 107 West operating between Lawrenceville and Danville.

The other trains operated by the A&D on its last day were No. 70, operating from Lawrenceville to Suffolk and return to Lawrenceville as Extra N&W 22 West; No. 69, operating from Pinners Point to Lawrenceville; and, Extra 104 East, operating from Danville to Lawrenceville.

The crew members of No. 70 were Engineer G. F. Fleming, Conductor A. B. Scott, Jr., Fireman B. E. Watson, Brakeman C. M. Moseley, and Flagman Glen Bollinger. Fireman M. G. Smith was with this crew securing mileage to qualify for engineer.

Train No. 69 was manned by Engineer E. E. Madray, Conductor C. J. Travis, Fireman C. E. Whitley, Brakeman M. R. Ballance and Flagman J. S. Jones.

The crew members of Extra 104 East were Engineer H. E. Pritchett, Conductor Arnold Barker, Fireman A. L. Arrington, Brakeman D. T. Clary, Jr. and Flagman Herman Connell.

On their next trip, these men would be the employees of a new railroad.

While the A&D was able to immediately upgrade its motive power to diesels for the new overnight service, it had inherited a railroad with a poor track structure. About 85 per cent of the railroad was laid with 70 to 75-pound rail and there was very little stone ballast. Only 60 per cent of the railroad was tie-plated. On the rest of the railroad the rails were fastened to the ties with fish plates, as was this section of track at Edgerton. (William E. Griffin, Jr. Collection)

As the tonnage increased, two diesels were required to handle the through freights. RS-2's Nos. 101 and 106 are handling a heavy eastbound Train No. 66 at Antlers on August 2, 1954. (William B. Gwaltney Photo/C. K. Marsh, Jr. Collection)

In a classic action shot, RS-2's Nos. 105 and 104 handle a freight on the line between Lawrenceville and Emporia in May of 1962. (J. Parker Lamb Photo)

Another view of RS-2's Nos. 105 and 104 with their train on the line between Lawrenceville and Emporia in May of 1962. In this view, the train rounds a curve on track that has been freshly ballasted. (J. Parker Lamb Photo)

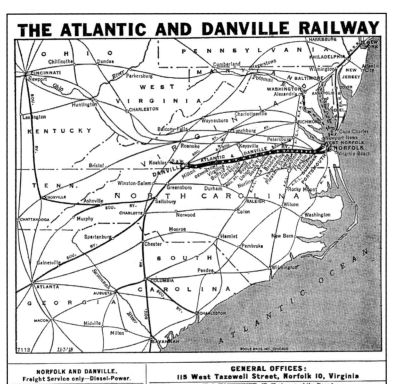

THE ATLANTIC AND DANVILLE RAILWAY

NORFOLK AND DANVILLE. Freight Service only—Diesel-Power.					
No. 85 Freight.	Mls.	January 1, 1953.			No. 86 Freight.
Daily		LEAVE	[ARRIVE]		Daily
10 01 P M	0	Norfolk[1]			5 40 A M
	0	Portsmouth[1]			
	0	Piners Point[2]			
	7.2	Boone			
10 56 "	18.8	Suffolk[3]			4 44 "
	30.9	Holland			
11 47 P M	39.0	Franklin[4]			3 53 "
	47.6	Courtland			
	55.0	Capron			
	61.1	Drewryville			
1 05 A M	74.8	Emporia[5]			2 35 "
	82.4	Pleasant Shade			
1 50 "	95.5	Lawrenceville			1 50 "
	108.5	Brodnax			
	112.3	La Crosse[6]			
2 59 "	115.2	South Hill			12 30 A M
	121.8	Union Level			
	125.2	Baskerville			
3 47 "	128.1	Antlers			11 50 P M
	131.0	Boydton			
	141.5	Jeffress[4]			
4 12 "	144.5	Clarksville			11 01 "
	148.8	Buffalo Junction			
	159.2	Virgilina			
	270.8	Deniston[7]			
	193.4	Milton			
6 40 A M	207.6	Danville[8]			8 45 P M
		ARRIVE	[LEAVE]		

WEST NORFOLK AND BOONE.				
	Mls.	STATIONS.		
Freight Service only.	0	West Norfolk		Freight Service only.
	3.4	Churchland		
	5.6	Boone		

GENERAL OFFICES:
115 West Tazewell Street, Norfolk 10, Virginia

H. C. HOFHEIMER, II, Chairman of the Board
L. D. CURTIS, President
E. R. BAIRD, Secretary-Treasurer
BAIRD, WHITE & LANNING, General Counsel
W. H. FLOWERS, Executive Assistant and Superintendent, Norfolk, Va.
W. F. POOLE, Engineer Maintenance of Way and Structures, Lawrenceville, Va.
J. P. HILLER, Auditor Disbursements
E. R. FREESLAND, Auditor Freight Accounts (Also O/C claims.)   Mrs. S. M. TAYLOR, Car Accountant
E. E. YOUNG, Traffic Manager, Norfolk, Va.
          (Also L. & D. claims.)
R. E. KRIEGER, Assistant to Traffic Manager, Norfolk, Va.
S. J. MUND, Executive Representative,
          5000 38th St., N. W., Washington, D. C.
W. A. RUSSELL, General Eastern Freight Agent,
          202S—500 Fifth Ave., New York 18, N.Y.
WALTER H. CANNER, Commercial Agent,   "   "
J. D. LOWE, General Southern Freight Agent,
          Room 606, 101 Marietta St. Bldg, Atlanta, Ga.
JOHN V. BENSON, General Agent,   "   "
W. E. BONNEY, Jr., Division Freight Agent,   "   "
          115 West Tazewell Street, Norfolk 10, Va.
E. C. CURLING, Commercial Agent,   "   "
IVOR A. PAGE, Commercial Agent,   "   "
ALEXANDER HAMILTON, General Agent,   "   "
          1045 Commercial Trust Bldg, Philadelphia, Pa.
JOSEPH B. RICHMOND, Jr., Gen. Agt., 650 Craghead St., Danville, Va.

Overnight Service between Hampton Roads, Va. (Norfolk - Portsmouth), and Danville, Va. A vital connecting Link between the East, South and Middle West.

Connections — [1]With C. & O., N. & W., N. S., P. R. R., Vgn. and N. & P. B. L. [2]With A. C. L., Sou. and N. & P. B. L. [3]With A. C. L., N. & W. and Vgn. [4]With S. A. L. [5]With A. C. L. [6]With Sou. [7]With N. & W. [8]With Carolina and Northwestern Ry. and Sou.

The Atlantic and Danville's listing in the April, 1956 Official Guide.

The old steam locomotive water tank was no longer needed by the A&D's motive power when this photo was taken on October 23, 1953 at the Lawrenceville yard. A&D RS-2's Nos. 105 and 101 await the next call to service. (Thomas Norrell Photo)

Eastbound Train No. 70 makes its morning departure from Lawrenceville with RS-2's Nos. 102 and 105 in the summer of 1960. (D. Courtney Griffin Photo)

RS-2 No. 101 crosses Main Street in South Hill in August of 1956 after spotting an LCL car on the house track. (James M. King Photo)

Having completed its switching chores at South Hill, the westbound local pulls up the grade departing town behind RS-2 No. 105. (Robert G. Lewis Photo)

We're still in the state of North Carolina as A&D Extra 104 East approaches Semora at Mile Post 184.4. Today, there is nothing to remind you of a railroad at this location. (Curt Tillotson, Jr. Photo)

The sun was beginning to disappear in the west on a brisk November afternoon in 1961 when Curt Tillotson caught A&D Extra 104 East rounding the curve at Milton, North Carolina with RS-2 No. 104 and RS-3 No. 107 and a 16-car train. (Curt Tillotson, Jr. Photo)

CHAPTER 4

THE NORFOLK, FRANKLIN, & DANVILLE - OPERATION BY THE NORFOLK & WESTERN RAILWAY
1962-1983

Ted Eudy, the NF&D's agent at Lawrenceville and longtime A&D employee, took this photo of the first train to be operated by the NF&D. Eastbound Train No. 70, with RS-2's Nos. 104 and 105, is shown setting off a pulpwood car at Edgerton for loading with the remainder of the train on the main line at right. The date was November 1, 1962 and the crew of this first NF&D train was comprised of Engineer E. E. Madray, Fireman C. E. Whitley, Conductor A. B. Scott, Jr., Brakeman Curtis M. Moseley and Flagman Glen Bollinger. (T. A. Eudy Photo/Fred Mullins Collection)

The Norfolk and Western undoubtedly saved the A&D from being dismantled in 1962. Judge Hoffman's order authorizing the sale of the company did not require that bidders be willing and able to continue operation of the railroad. Any interested person or corporation with the money could be a potential buyer and that included junk dealers who might want to tear up the railroad for its scrap value. Fortunately, when the public auction was held on September 28, 1962, the N&W was the only bidder.

The N&W and the A&D's trustee had reached an agreement on July 30, 1962 that in the event of a sale, the N&W would bid $1.5 million in cash to purchase the bankrupt railroad. The N&W also agreed that it would spend the money necessary to keep the line in operation.

At that time, the N&W already owned more than 45 percent of the A&D's outstanding first mortgage bonds and 12 percent of the second mortgage bonds. The A&D also owed the N&W approximately $200,000 representing the balance due on conditional sale contracts covering the sale to the A&D of 164 boxcars and pulpwood cars and two diesel locomotives.

Pursuant to the terms of the July 30 agreement, the A&D's trustee petitioned the bankruptcy court for an order approving execution of the agreement and directing the sale of the property. On July 31, Judge Hoffman approved the agreement and directed the preparation of an order of sale.

The sale was ordered on August 18 following a hearing in which the court found that it was not economically feasible for the A&D to continue operations as an independent company; that the railroad could not be successfully reorganized; and, that an appropriate disposition of the A&D's affairs would be the sale of the property at public auction.

The sale was held on September 28 and, in accordance with its agreement, the N&W bid $1.5 million for the properties of the A&D. However, the purchase of the A&D was subject to final approval of the Interstate Commerce Commission and the court ordered the A&D's trustee to continue operation of the line pending conclusion of the conveyance.

The N&W immediately announced plans to rehabilitate the A&D and operate it as a wholly-owned subsidiary. The N&W also announced that it was renaming the road the "Norfolk, Franklin and Danville Railway Company". The new company was incorporated under the laws of the Commonwealth of Virginia on October 2, 1962 for the purpose of acquiring the assets and operating the line of the railroad of the former A&D. The articles of incorporation authorized the issuance of 20,000 shares of common stock at par value of $100 each.

On October 3, 1962, the N&W assigned all of its rights and obligations under the bid to the NF&D and by order of the court dated October 4, 1962, the acceptance of the bid of the N&W was confirmed.

Also on October 4, the N&W and NF&D made a joint application to the Interstate Commerce Commission requesting authority for the N&W to acquire control of the NF&D through stock ownership; for the NF&D to acquire the lines of railroad and property of the former A&D, including trackage rights over the Southern Railway between Jeffress and Clarksville Junction; and, for the NF&D to acquire trackage rights over the approximately 26.59 miles of N&W main line between Suffolk and Lamberts Point, Norfolk County, Virginia.

By separate application, the NF&D sought authority from the ICC to issue not exceeding 20,000 shares of common stock of par value of $100 each. The entire 20,000 shares were to be issued to the N&W for $2 million in cash. The stock issue was authorized by the NF&D's Board of Directors on October 3, 1962 and on that same date the N&W subscribed to the entire issue. Hence, all NF&D stock was owned by the N&W. The proceeds from the sale of the stock were used for the purchase of the assets of the A&D and for working capital.

Also by separate application the A&D sought authority to abandon operation over the line of the Atlantic Coast Line Railroad between Boone and Pinners Point. Trackage rights over the ACL to Pinners Point would be not required by the NF&D as the

THE TIME SHOWN CONVEYS NO TIMETABLE AUTHORITY

THIRD CLASS 85 Ex. Sun.	Capacity of Tracks in cars		TIMETABLE NUMBER ONE EFFECTIVE 12:01 A.M. FEBRUARY 1, 1967 STATIONS		Miles from Suffolk	Station Numbers	THIRD CLASS 86 Ex. Sun.
	Siding	Other					
A.M.			Lv.				P.M.
10:00	35	Yard	SUFFOLK	D	....	18	10:45
			7.7				
10:20	....	5	LUMMIS		7.7	25	10:30
			4.3				
10:30	40	15	HOLLAND		12.0	29	10:20
			8.2				
11:15	35	30	FRANKLIN	D	20.2	38	10:00
			2.5				
11:20	35	....	HUNTERDALE		22.7	40	9:30
			3.0				
11:30	....	3	STORY		25.7	43	9:20
			3.0				
11:45	32	16	COURTLAND	D	28.7	46	9:10
			5.5				
11:59	....	3	POPE		34.2	52	8:55
			2.0				
12:10	....	29	CAPRON		36.2	54	8:45
			6.3				
12:20	....	8	DREWRYVILLE		42.5	60	8:30
			4.9				
12:30	....	8	ADAMS GROVE		47.4	65	8:20
			3.8				
12:37	....	3	GREEN PLAIN		51.2	68	8:10
			5.0				
1:15	....	Yard	EMPORIA	D	56.2	73	8:00
			7.6				
1:30	....	6	PLEASANT SHADE		63.8	81	6:45
			7.9				
2:00	25	....	EDGERTON		71.7	89	6:25
			5.1				
2:25	50	Yard	LAWRENCEVILLE	D	76.8	94	6:00
P.M.			Ar.	Lv.			P.M.

THE TIME SHOWN CONVEYS NO TIMETABLE AUTHORITY

THIRD CLASS 85 Ex. Sun.	Capacity of Tracks in Cars		TIMETABLE NUMBER ONE EFFECTIVE 12:01 A.M. FEBRUARY 1, 1967 STATIONS		Miles From Suffolk	Station No.	THIRD CLASS 86 Ex. Sun.
	Siding	Other					
P.M.			Lv.				P.M.
5:00	50	Yard	LAWRENCEVILLE	D	76.8	94	4:45
			13.1				
5:25	....	8	BRODNAX		89.9	107	4:15
			3.8				
5:45	....	10	LA CROSSE		93.7	111	4:00
			2.9				
6:15	25	Yard	SOUTH HILL	D	96.6	114	3:30
			6.5				
6:35	....	8	UNION LEVEL		103.1	120	2:45
			3.4				
6:45	....	6	BASKERVILLE		106.5	124	2:30
			2.9				
7:00	25	3	ANTLERS		109.4	127	2:15
			4.1				
7:20	....	8	BOYDTON		113.5	131	2:00
			6.9				
7:40	....	15	FINCHLEY		120.4	138	1:45
			2.7				
7:50	22	....	JEFFRESS		123.1	140	1:30
			2.6				
8:05	....	20	CLARKSVILLE	D	125.7	143	1:15
			0.3				
8:10	....	....	CLARKSVILLE JCT.		126.0	...	1:01
			4.3				
8:20	....	13	BUFFALO JUNCTION		130.3	147	12:55
			5.5				
8:35	....	23	NELSON		135.8	153	12:45
			4.9				
8:50	....	28	VIRGILINA		140.7	158	12:30
			7.5				
9:05	....	8	MAYO		148.2	165	12:15
			4.1				
9:30	....	25	DENNISTON		152.3	169	11:45
			4.4				
9:45	....	10	ALTON		156.7	174	11:15
			10.5				
10:00	....	15	SEMORA		167.2	184	11:00
			6.7				
10:15	....	12	MILTON		173.9	191	10:45
			5.9				
10:30	....	22	BLANCHE		179.8	197	10:30
			5.3				
10:45	....	8	EAST DANVILLE		185.1	202	10:00
			2.5				
11:30	30	Yard	DANVILLE	D	187.6	205	9:30
P.M.			Ar.	Lv.			A.M.

NF&D timetable No. 1, February 1, 1967.

THE TIME SHOWN CONVEYS NO TIMETABLE AUTHORITY

THIRD CLASS 69 Ex. Sun.	Capacity of Tracks in Cars		TIMETABLE NUMBER ONE EFFECTIVE 12:01 A.M. FEBRUARY 1, 1967 STATIONS		Miles from Suffolk	Station Numbers	THIRD CLASS 70 Ex. Sun.
	Siding	Other					
P.M.			Lv.				A.M.
2:30	20	Yard	WEST NORFOLK		17.3	0	10:30
			3.4				
2:45	....	6	CHURCHLAND		13.9	3	10:15
			2.6				
3:00	....	8	BOONE		11.3	6	10:00
			11.3				
3:45	35	Yard	SUFFOLK		....	18	9:15
P.M.			Ar.	Lv.			A.M.

new railroad would have access to the Norfolk and Portsmouth Belt Line Railroad and the N&W's Norfolk terminal by virtue of the trackage rights arrangement to Lamberts Point. Under such an arrangement the NF&D did not have to use the interlocking at Boone, an expensive operation, and avoided the Pinners Point terminal costs that had been so burdensome to the A&D. Under the NF&D operation the line between Suffolk and West Norfolk once again reverted to branch line status.

On October 29, 1962, the ICC approved all of the transactions involved in the NF&D's takeover and operation of the former A&D. The railroad began operation under the new ownership of the NF&D on November 1, 1962. The first train operated by the NF&D was eastbound No. 70 on November 1 with the crew of Engineer E. E. Madray, Conductor A. B. Scott, Jr., Fireman C. E. Whitley, Brakeman C. M. Moseley and Flagman Glen Bollinger.

Charles G. Hammond, Jr., formerly Superintendent of the N&W's Radford Division, was elected Vice President and General Manager of the NF&D. Hammond served as the railroad's Chief Operating Officer, reporting to Stuart T. Saunders, President of both the NF&D and the N&W. Members of the NF&D's Board of Directors were Mr. Saunders, John P. Fishwick, N&W Vice President-Law, and Robert B. Claytor, N&W General Solicitor.

The headquarters for the NF&D's Operating Department was established at 181 South Main Street in Suffolk on November 12. The new railroad's administrative personnel were located at the N&W's general office building in Roanoke. Day to day operations were directed by Superintendent William C. Markert, a former A&D transportation officer, whose office was located at the division headquarters in Lawrenceville.

At the western end of the railroad, the NF&D's line entered

While administrative and financial functions were performed for the NF&D by personnel located in the N&W's general office building at Roanoke, operations were directed by transportation department located in the NF&D office building located at 181 South Main Street in Suffolk. (William E. Griffin, Jr. Photo)

Danville from the east and retained the A&D's connection with the Southern Railway main line just south of the Southern's Dan River Bridge. A spur line extended north approximately one mile along the Dan River. Two tracks paralleling the NF&D spur were used for receiving and making up road trains and constituted NF&D's only yard facility at Danville. Interchange between the Southern and the NF&D was handled by each road delivering to interchange tracks near the Southern's passenger station in downtown Danville.

The major commodities transported by the NF&D were paper and related products, tires and crude rubber, and chemicals. Three major shippers - Union Camp at Franklin, Goodyear at Danville, and Virginia Chemicals at West Norfolk - accounted for most of these commodities. The NF&D also handled commodities such as farm products, crude petroleum, natural gas, lumber and wood products, stone, clay and glass products, and waste and scrap materials. During most of the company's history, shippers located along the 40-mile segment of the railroad between Franklin and West Norfolk accounted for over 50 percent of the NF&D's traffic.

While no substantial economies were anticipated in the operation of the NF&D, the N&W believed that the rehabilitated railroad and improved service would attract sufficient additional revenues to enable the NF&D to earn a fair return on investment. In fact, the N&W did realize a handsome return on its investment in the NF&D. In E. F. Pat Striplin's book, The Norfolk and Western: A History (published by the railroad in 1981), John P. Fishwick was quoted as describing the N&W's purchase of the A&D as "... the best buy we ever made. We make more than the purchase price in an average year now".

Many of the N&W's resources, such as its system-wide industrial development program, were made available to the NF&D. With the N&W's backing, the NF&D was able to attract a number of significant indus-

Following its acquisition of the A&D, the N&W announced that it would spend more than $1 million to improve the roadbed, tracks and facilities. Funds for the rehabilitation of the line would be advanced to the NF&D by the N&W. This NF&D track force is pictured surfacing track near Franklin in March of 1963. In the picture, Foreman C. C. Crickenberger is checking on raising the track with a surfacing scope. In the background is a multiple tie tamping machine operated by Charles Parker. Others in the photo are (from left to right) Roadmaster Fred Duncan and Trackmen J. H. Stith and Gray Boykins. (William E. Griffin, Jr. Collection)

The NF&D commenced operations with two new diesels. Prior to its demise, the A&D had returned RS-2's Nos. 101 and 102 to Alco for remanufacture in accordance with the specifications for a DL-701 (RS-36) 1800-horsepower road switcher locomotive. These new diesels were subject to a conditional sales agreement obligation that the N&W agreed to assume in its bid to purchase the A&D. In October of 1962 the two RS-36's (Numbered the 1 and 2) were delivered bearing the A&D's name and paint scheme. The two locomotives are shown on the ready track at Danville in November of 1962. (Curt Tillotson, Jr. Photo)

tries to locate their plants on its line. In 1963, Kingsberry Homes Corporation built a new $650,00 plant on 44 acres just west of Emporia. Lumber, plywood and gypsum board was shipped by rail to the industry for the production of manufactured homes. In December of that year, the NF&D began construction of a new combination freight station and office building at Franklin (the only one it would ever build) to replace the old warehouse-ticket office on Little Street and the nearby freight station that had been used since 1886. The new Franklin facility was a modified version of a Kingsberry Homes residence. In May of 1965, U. S. Gypsum Co. began construction of a multi-million dollar hardboard manufacturing plant on the NF&D two miles southeast of Danville. In December of 1965, the Georgia-Pacific Corporation's new plywood plant, which was located on 60 acres of property at Emporia, went into full operation providing the NF&D with shipments of plywood and wood chips. Finally, in December of 1966, the Goodyear Tire & Rubber Co. began construction of a multi-million dollar plant about one mile south of Danville in Pittsylvania County. This plant went into full operation in 1967 and provided much traffic to the NF&D.

However, in the early 1960's much work was required to rehabilitate the railroad. Stuart T. Saunders, N&W's President, stated to the press that $1 million would be spent to improve the road-bed, tracks and other facilities, and $800,000 more would be spent immediately for operating equipment. Funds for the rehabilitation and operation of the line were obtained by the NF&D through advances from the N&W.

While most of the former A&D equipment was in poor condition, the NF&D did inherit two practically new diesel locomotives from its predecessor. Prior to its demise, the A&D had returned Alco RS-2 1500-h.p. diesels 101 and 102 to the builder's factory in Schenectady, New York for remanufacture in accordance with the specifications for a DL-701 (RS-36) 1800-h.p. road switcher locomotive. The remanufacture of the locomotives was subject to a conditional sales agreement dated August 1, 1962, an obligation that the N&W agreed to assume in its bid to purchase the A&D. The two remanufactured locomotives, in the A&D's paint scheme and bearing road numbers 1 and 2, were delivered in October of 1962. Subsequently, the units were repainted blue (then black) with white lettering for NF&D service and were the "workhorses" of the railroad's motive power fleet for twenty years. All of the former A&D diesels received the new NF&D monogram in 1963 after receiving complete paint jobs at the N&W shops in Roanoke.

Former A&D diesels 103-107 remained in service until the mid-1960's. When they were retired, the N&W sold four former Nickel Plate Railroad 1800-h.p. Alco RS-11's to the NF&D. Renumbered NF&D 201-204, the units worked on the railroad until retired in 1980-81. While the NF&D owned only six locomotives, its normal operations regularly required eleven to fourteen units and the remainder were provided by the N&W under a locomotive lease arrangement. The N&W leased 4-axle, 1700 to 1800 h.p.

A&D RS-2 No. 106 was never returned to service. The other RS-2's (Nos. 103, 104 and 105) and RS-3 No. 107 became NF&D locomotives. They initially retained the A&D paint scheme, the A&D name removed from their carbodies and with the new NF&D logo added below the cab windows. RS-2 No. 104 is at Suffolk on September 26, 1964. (J. H. Wade Photo/F. E. Ardrey, Jr. Collection)

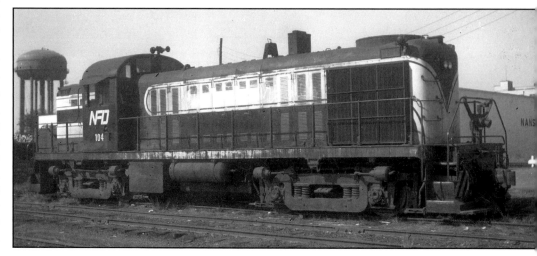

locomotives to the NF&D for a monthly rental charge of $900 per unit. Over the years, many N&W Alco T-6 switchers and EMD GP-9's and GP-18's were assigned to handle the trains over the NF&D.

The N&W also assisted its new subsidiary to supplement the aged and poorly maintained rolling stock fleet of the former A&D. In 1967, arrangements were made to sell the NF&D a group of two hundred 50-foot, 50-ton, double door steel box-cars that had become surplus to the needs of the Nickel Plate, another N&W subsidiary. These cars were rebuilt at the N&W's Decatur shops and were painted boxcar red with white stenciling. Numbered 2300-2499, they carried the same slanted NF&D logo that had been applied to the cabs of the diesel locomotives. As the result of a N&W business arrangement with the Central Railroad Company of New Jersey, the NF&D also became the owner of another 200 boxcars that never carried the company's reporting marks. In 1967, the then-bankrupt CNJ was in need of boxcars. At that time, the N&W had 200 50-ton 50-foot double-door class B-4 boxcars in storage pending retirement. The N&W determined that the cars could be refurbished at minimal cost and entered into an arrangement to lease the cars to the CNJ through its NF&D subsidiary. The N&W advanced the full pur-chase price of the cars to the NF&D. The cars were rebuilt in the N&W shops at Brewster, Ohio and were leased by the NF&D to the CNJ. Numbered 25000-25199, the lease of the cars to the CNJ generated a substantial cash flow to the NF&D of nearly $12,000 per month. The NF&D owned only two cabooses. Numbered 112 and 113, they were all steel 34-foot N&W class CG cabooses. The N&W also leased a number of caboose cars in its series CF, C30 and C30A to the NF&D. The leased cabooses were not stenciled for the NF&D and carried their N&W markings and numbers dur-ing operation by the subsidiary road.

The N&W also spent more than $800,000 on new operating equipment for the NF&D. This included the acquisi-tion of four former Nickle Plate Railroad 1800-horsepower RS-11's to replace the former A&D RS-2's and RS-3 when they were retired. RS-11 No. 201 is shown with RS-36 No. 1 at Lawrenceville in July of 1970. (Tom L. Sink Photo)

Train operations were slow over most of the NF&D. The re-habilitated roadway was still laid with light rail and surface kinks made for a rough ride. West of Lawrenceville, the rail was pre-dominately 75-pound with some 80-pound and 85-pound relay rail that had been laid by the A&D. Train speed was restricted to 25 m.p.h. over most of the line with restrictions of 10 m.p.h. in some locations.

The traffic handled on the eastern end of the railroad required better track conditions and by the late-1970's the NF&D was laying sections of welded rail east of Lawrenceville. From West Norfolk to Suffolk, the NF&D laid sections of 110 to 112-pound welded rail. West of Suffolk, welded rail was laid to M. P. 66 at Courtland. From Courtland to just west of Adams Grove, there were sections of 85-pound and 90-pound relay rail, then 85-pound and 90-pound welded rail from Emporia to the rock quarry of Vulcan Materials at Edgerton. A short section of 112-pound welded rail was laid for two miles east of the Vulcan Materials facility.

In the 1960's, the NF&D operated five freight trains daily ex-cept Sunday. There were two through trains, one in each direction between Suffolk and Danville. A turnaround local operated six days a week between Suffolk and West Norfolk, and there were two local assignments - one be-tween Suffolk and Franklin and another between Lawrenceville and Suffolk. The through ser-vice came to an end in the early 1970's with the passage of a new Hours of Service Law that lim-ited train and engine crews to 12 hours of continuous service.

Thereafter, NF&D operations were centered at Lawrenceville. Turnaround locals were oper-ated from Lawrenceville on a

This NF&D agency facility was located at the former A&D yard at Danville. This photo of the agency was taken on May 29, 1982. (Curt Tillotson, Jr. Photo)

RS-36 No. 2, shown here with RS-2 No. 103 on an eastbound freight near Capron in the winter of 1966, retains its A&D paint scheme. However, RS-2 No. 103 has been repainted in N&W blue, the only RS-2 to receive that treatment. (Jim Shaw Photo)

The traffic density on the western end of the railroad has always been light. The bulk of the traffic handled on this section was either originated or terminated in the Danville area. With the exception of the Danville traffic most of the carloads were generated by one shipper - D&D Pulpwood at Nelson. This pulpwood yard accounted for 80 percent of the outbound carloads. The inbound traffic to the west end was primarily fertilizer to various points, lumber and steel beams to Virginia Homes at Boydton, and sand to Felton Brothers at Finchley and the Virginia Department of Highways at Buffalo Junction.

six day a week basis to Suffolk and Danville. Road switchers and locals continued to be operated from Lawrenceville, Danville, Suffolk and Franklin. The Danville switcher operated six days a week to perform all yard and interchange work and serve industries at Danville and East Danville. The Lawrenceville switcher handled local work between Lawrenceville and Emporia and the Franklin switcher's main responsibility was to work the Union Camp plant at Franklin. One Suffolk switcher handled the interchange work and served industries while the other handled the local work between Suffolk and West Norfolk.

In the late 1970's, the NF&D used two different schemes of train operations on the west end, depending upon the traffic requirements of the line. When there was a decline in business the NF&D operated a Lawrenceville/Danville tri-weekly local, operating westbound on Monday, Wednesday and Friday, eastbound on Tuesday, Thursday and Saturday. When traffic increased, the NF&D operated a Lawrenceville to Denniston turnaround local and a Danville to Denniston turnaround local six days a week.

With its poor track conditions and light traffic density, the NF&D's west end was a prime candidate for abandonment if the N&W could find another way to re-route the overhead traffic. An opportunity to do so was created with the merger of the N&W and the Southern Railway.

On June 2, 1980, the N&W and Southern announced that they would seek approval from their board of directors to consolidate ownership and control of the two railroads under a single holding company (originally NWS Enterprises, later renamed the Norfolk Southern Corporation). On July 22, 1980, the boards of both companies approved the merger and the N&W promptly announced its intention to abandon that portion of the NF&D which extended from Mile Post 113.9 at South Hill to the line's western terminus at Danville, a total of 90.6 miles.

The town of South Hill offered the most opposition to the proposed abandonment. It feared that the loss of rail access would seriously reduce the development potential of industrial properties

In the early days of NF&D operations, RS-3 No. 107 is shown with a freight train near Franklin in 1963. (W. B. Gwaltney Photo/ C. K. Marsh, Jr. Collection)

F&D RS-11 No. 203 and two N&W T-6's roll an eastbound freight train at Semora, North Carolina n March 11, 1978. (Bob Graham Photo)

es. On September 17, 1980, the NF&D advised that the eastern erminus of the proposed abandonment would be changed to Mile Post 117.0 to keep South Hill's industrial sites within the opera-ional portion of the line.

On November 3, 1980, the N&W published its notice of intent o file for abandonment of a portion of the NF&D as a part of its pplication for merger with the Southern Railway. In that notice, he western terminus of the proposed abandonment was changed o a point just east of Blanche, North Carolina. The abandonment vas to be from Mile Post 117.0, approximately 3.1 miles west of outh Hill, to Mile Post 196.9, approximately 0.2 miles east of Blanche, a total of 79.8 miles. This included approximately 2.24 niles of trackage rights over the Southern Railway between Mile Post 140.4, Jeffress, and Mile Post 142.7, Clarksville. It also in-luded approximately 0.79 mile of joint trackage owned by the NF&D and Southern between Mile Post 142.7, Clarksville, and Mile Post 143.5, Clarksville Junction.

If the N&W/Southern affiliation was approved, it was pro-osed that the overhead traffic that had moved over the abandoned ection of the NF&D would be re-routed over alternate N&W and Southern lines. Traffic that had moved over-ead on the NF&D from Danville to points east of South Iill would be re-routed via the Southern to an interchange vith the N&W at either Lynchburg or Burkeville, Virgin-a, thence to Suffolk for interchange with the NF&D and novement to destination. Traffic that had moved over-ead on the NF&D from Danville to an interchange with he N&W at Denniston would be re-routed via the South-rn from Danville to an interchange with the N&W at ither Altavista or Lynchburg. Westbound traffic would nove via the reverse route.

It was also proposed that Southern would acquire the emaining 8 miles of the NF&D from Mile Post 196.9 at Blanche westward to the end of the NF&D in Danville at Mile Post 204.9, including the NF&D spur along the Dan River. After the acquisition, the Southern would serve ll former NF&D shippers at Blanche, East Danville and Danville with a road switcher assignment operated out of Dundee Yard at Danville.

The petition for abandonment of the NF&D from

South Hill, Virginia to Blanche, North Caro-lina was filed with the ICC on December 4, 1980 as a part of the application by NWS Enterprises, Inc. for control of the N&W and Southern. The abandonment proposal was conditioned upon the Commission's approv-al of the merger application.

On March 25, 1982, the ICC issued its approval of the Norfolk Southern Corpora-tion's control of the N&W and Southern. The Commission's approval of the NF&D aban-donment petition was issued concurrently with the merger decision. Upon receipt of the ICC's approval to abandon the track be-tween South Hill and Blanche, the decision was made to effect the abandonment on June 1, 1982.

As a result of the abandonment, the N&W abolished one job - the NF&D's Law-renceville-Danville Local. The last NF&D train left Danville on May 28, 1982. Ap-propriately, the consist of the last train was led by NF&D RS-36 No. 2, followed by N&W GP-9 No. 3487 and N&W T-6 No. 44. The NF&D agency in Danville was also closed and the work was transferred to the Southern's agency at the Danville passenger sta-tion. Since the Southern's Dundee Yard had sufficient capacity to handle additional traffic, the yard tracks of the NF&D at Danville were used by the Southern for the storage of freight cars. Soon, the salvage crews began the work of dismantling the 79.8 miles of main line.

Following the abandonment of the line from Blanche to South Hill, the NF&D's operations were centered at Suffolk. Tri-weekly local service was operated between Suffolk and South Hill and a turnaround local operated between Suffolk and West Norfolk three days per week. Also, a road switcher operated at Franklin seven days a week and could operate as needed from Franklin to Suffolk or Emporia, and return.

The following year the separate corporate identity of the NF&D would come to an end.

One of the NF&D's best shippers was the Vulcan Materials quarry at M. P. 86.8, near Edgerton. Vulcan Materials is the nation's largest producer of construction aggregates, primarily crushed stone, sand and gravel for use in construction and the building and maintaining of roads. The NF&D operated a dedicated rock train to quarry and here we see RS-36 No. 2 delivering empties to the quarry for loading. (Ed Sharpe Photo)

RS-36 No. 1 and RS-1 No. 203 are on the N&W mainline at Suffolk setting out cars from Empo ria for interchange to th N&W. The date is Apr 1, 1977. (Bob Grahar Photo)

N&W diesel locomotives were handling more and more of the the NF&D assignments when this photo of the Lawrenceville locomotive facility was photographed in April of 1970. From left to right are N&W GP-9 No. 865, N&W RS-11 No. 390 and NF&D RS-11 No. 201. (Stanley W. Short Photo)

NF&D RS-11 No. 201 pul its eastbound train out the yard and prepares stop at the Lawrencevill freight station. Crews o erating trains originatin at Lawrenceville were re quired to receive a Clea ance Card from the on-du operator before departin with their train. (Stanley V Short Photo)

Westbound Train No. 85 nears the end of its run at Danville on April 19, 1980. On this day, the 41-car train is being handled by NF&D RS-11 No. 204 and N&W T-6 No. 36. Curt Tillotson, Jr. Photo)

Alco 1000-horsepower T-6 class switchers frequently worked NF&D assignments with the N&W eventually leasing four of the units to its subsidiary. "Leased to NF&D" was stenciled under the cab number on these leased units. These locomotives worked the "Goodyear Switcher" at Danville, the West Norfolk Switcher and mainline in combination with other NF&D and N&W power. T-6 No. 49 and another T-6 are on the NF&D ready track at Danville as T-6 No. 30 passes with a cut of cars on July 11, 1981. (Curt Tillotson, Jr. Photo)

NF&D Train No. 85 was assigned all N&W power (GP-9 No. 3486, T-6 No. 36 and GP-9 No. 3489) as it passes the old Milton, North Carolina depot with its 61-car train on May 30, 1981. (Curt Tillotson, Jr. Photo)

NF&D Train No. 85 again with all N&W power. On May 23, 1981, motive power for the 40-car train is provided by N&W GP-9's Nos. 740 and 3489 and T-6 No. 36.. (Curt Tillotson, Jr. Photo)

The end was fast approaching for both the "Deuce" and NF&D when the locomotive was photographed on the West Norfolk Switcher at Suffolk on February 21, 1983. (William E. Griffin, Jr. Photo)

As the last operating A&D locomotive, perhaps it was only fitting that the "Deuce" would lead the locomotive consist of the NF&D's last train to operate from Danville. Photographed on the ready track and ready for the last run on May 28, 1982 is NF&D RS-36 No. 2, N&W GP-9 No. 3487 and N&W T-6 No. 44. (Ed Fielding Photo)

CHAPTER 5

THE FRANKLIN DISTRICT OF THE NORFOLK AND WESTERN - OPERATION BY NORFOLK SOUTHERN CORPORATION
1983 - PRESENT

On December 30, 1983, the separate corporate identity of the NF&D came to an end. On that date, the NF&D was merged with its parent company and was thereafter operated as the Franklin District of the N&W's Norfolk Division.

Initially, the Franklin District was comprised of 116.9 miles of mainline track between West Norfolk and South Hill and was operated by the N&W in a manner similar to its operation of the NF&D. Operations were centered at Suffolk where connection was made with the N&W's main line and traffic could be interchanged with the Seaboard System Railroad at Suffolk, Franklin, Emporia and LaCrosse. Train service consisted of two turnaround local freights and one stone train.

The "West Norfolk Job" was called at Suffolk at 9 a.m. and normally made a round trip to the Virginia Chemicals plant at West Norfolk and return to Suffolk each Monday, Wednesday and Friday. Typically, the train operated with one locomotive, a caboose and seven to ten freight cars. Additional trains were operated to and from the plant when required by the business.

The "Stone Train" was called at Suffolk between 6 and 7 p.m. and operated each day Monday through Friday. The train departed Suffolk with empty stone hoppers and ran to the Vulcan Materials quarry at Edgerton. Upon arrival at Edgerton, the train set out the empties and picked up the loads that had been spotted by the

industry's employees. The train then ran all the way to N&W's Portlock Yard in Norfolk where it dropped the loads and picked up the empties for the next day's stone train to Edgerton. The train then returned to Suffolk with the empties where the crew went off duty.

The "NF&D Local" operated six days a week on a varying schedule. On Mondays, the train was called at Suffolk at 11 a.m. and made a round trip from Suffolk to Franklin or Courtland and return. On Tuesdays and Thursdays, the train was called at Suffolk between 10 and 11 a.m. and made a trip from Suffolk to Lawrenceville/South Hill, where it tied up for the night. This train could be required to make a Suffolk to Boone turn before heading west. On Wednesdays and Fridays, the train was called at Lawrenceville/South Hill between 10 and 11 a.m. and made the return trip to Suffolk. On Saturdays, the train was called at Suffolk between 8 and 8:30 a. m. and made a round trip from Suffolk to Franklin or Emporia and return.

The principal shippers located on the Franklin District were Virginia Chemicals at West Norfolk, Union Camp (paper products) at Franklin, Georgia Pacific (plywood and wood chips) at Emporia, and Vulcan Materials (stone) at Edgerton. Pulpwood, brick, fertilizer, peanuts and miscellaneous agricultural products were shipped to and from the various stations at Suffolk, Holland, Courtland, Capron, Lawrenceville, LaCrosse and South Hill.

Following the abandonment of the NF&D line between South Hill, Va. and Blanche, N.C., former NF&D customers at Blanche, East Danville and Danville were served by the Southern Railway from its Dundee Yard at Danville. In this photograph, the "Goodyear Switcher", with GP-38 No. 2798 and U23B No. 3959, is shown as it returns from switching the Goodyear tire plant on the former NF&D main line east of Danville. The train is on the old NF&D-Southern connection track. The old NF&D yard, now used only for the storage of cars, is in the background and the Southern's main line and passenger station is about 100 yards behind the photographer. This photo was taken in November of 1983. (Curt Tillotson, Jr. Photo)

It's November of 1984 and Southern Railway power has now been replaced by Norfolk Southern power on the "Goodyear Switcher". The train is on the former A&D/NF&D main line east of Danville and is backing its train to Dundee Yard after working the Goodyear tire plant. Two GP-38-2's (No. 5036 and 5032) provide the motive power for the afternoon train. (Curt Tillotson, Jr. Photo)

In the years following the NF&D's merger into the N&W, loaded cars handled over the Franklin District increased each year and, by 1986, the loads handled (27,029) were almost twice those handled in 1983 (14,894). However, while stone shipped from Vulcan Materials accounted for the majority of the loads, almost half of the revenue earned on the Franklin District was derived from the traffic handled to and from Franklin.

In recognition of the importance of the Franklin business, the N&W established a Suffolk to Franklin Turn, identified in the N&W numbering system as local freight N27S69. The other former NF&D locals were also given numbers in the N&W system. The West Norfolk Turn became N20S69; the stone train became N25S69, and the NF&D local became N23S69.

These trains, as well as all other former N&W and Southern

trains, were renumbered effective January 1, 1988, when the new "Norfolk Southern Unique Train and Yard Run Numbering System" was placed in service. Since 1982 the N&W and Southern had retained their pre-merger schemes of identifying train and yard movements. This had required Norfolk Southern to maintain two separate sets of computer logic to handle the different formats. In 1987, when Norfolk Southern realigned its operating divisions and updated its system-wide computer network, it resolved this situation by creating a new numbering system. Under the new system, all Norfolk Southern train movements were identified by a "number" that was unique to the train's movement over a particular territory. Line segment codes were developed for the various Norfolk Southern territories over which trains operated. The Suffolk-West Norfolk Turn became Norfolk Southern train N30N4. The Suffolk-

Having completed the yard switching at Lawrenceville, Locomotive Engineer Percy Wilkins stops the NF&D Local just short of the road crossing at the freight station to pick up any final orders before departing for the return trip to Suffolk. The date is November 16, 1988 and the motive power for the local is provided by Norfolk and Western GP-35 No. 1325 and GP-38AC No. 4150. (William E. Griffin, Jr. Photo)

Franklin Turn became train N07N4. The stone train, with limits between Suffolk and Portlock, became the N47N1. When operated between Suffolk and South Hill, the local was identified as N31N4. When operating between South Hill and Suffolk, it was designated as the N32N4.

More significant changes would occur on the Franklin District in the late-1980's as Norfolk Southern Corporation continued the process of consolidating its two properties into one transportation company. By 1986, Norfolk Southern had given up on its unsuccessful attempt to purchase control of the Consolidated Rail Corporation (Conrail) and began to focus on the task of eliminating low-density mileage from the 17,000-mile system created by the merger of the N&W and Southern. From a 1987 review of its property, Norfolk Southern had determined that the system contained about 2,700 miles of low-volume lines. While some of these lines were clearly candidates for abandonment, NS concluded that certain of the lines possessed the potential to be operated as short line railroads.

Class I railroads had been given greater flexibility to dispose of unproductive lines as a result of the reduced

On February 3, 1989, the Interstate Commerce Commission approved the Norfolk Southern's application to abandon the 21.8 miles of line between South Hill and Lawrenceville. The "official" last run from South Hill occurred on March 15, 1989 with GP-20 No. 2008, three freight cars and N&W caboose 555074. Norfolk Southern Agent-General Yardmaster H. R. Hogan, the Lawrenceville mayor and a newspaper reporter rode on the front to the locomotive all the way from South Hill to Lawrenceville. This photograph of the final run was taken as the train passed through Charlie Hope, Virginia about 5 miles west of Lawrenceville. The author's mother had boarded Southern Railway passenger trains at Charlie Hope in 1925-26 for Suffolk traveling to her job as a school teacher at Chuckatuck, Virginia and in 1927-28 when she traveled to Pinners Point enroute to her teaching assignments on the Eastern Shore. My grandfather would hitch up the horse and buggy at the nearby farm where my mother was born and raised and took her to the little one-room Charlie Hope station, flagging down the train for her to board. It seemed the fitting place for the author to photograph the last train over the line. (William E. Griffin, Jr. Photo)

A "cleanup trip" to South Hill was made two weeks after the "official last run" with GP20 No. 2008 and N&W caboose 555028 to pick up three empty cars that had been left in South Hill. The last train ever to operate from South Hill departed on the morning of March 29, 1989 for the return trip to Lawrenceville. In this photo, the crew members of this last train pose with their locomotive prior to departure. From left to right they are Engineer R. L. Capps, Conductor J. E. Presson and Brakemen William Moody and Nat Blanton. (South Hill Enterprise Photo)

federal regulations contained in the Staggers Rail Act of 1980. However, while other Class I railroads had either abandoned or sold their marginally profitable lines, Norfolk Southern developed an innovative strategy to lease the lines to short line operators. In 1987, Norfolk Southern created the "Thoroughbred Short Line Program". Under this program, low-density lines were leased to short line operators who could cater to the individual needs of low-volume customers. These short lines also served as feeder-lines to Norfolk Southern, which provided dependable service over the long haul for the short line's shippers. Norfolk Southern also provided the feeder line with marketing and pricing support, technical assistance in areas such as electronic data interchange and customer freight billing. If the short line was successful, the operators could receive credits on their lease and were given an opportunity to purchase the line at its net liquidation value. If the short line

Norfolk Southern GP-38AC No. 4143 and GP20 No. 2008 prepare to depart Lawrenceville with the Local in December of 1989. The Lawrenceville agency was closed by Norfolk Southern on March 19, 1990 and in 1991 the freight station was dismantled piece by piece and the materials sold to create an addition to a private home at a ski resort in Banner-Elk, North Carolina. (William E. Griffin, Jr. Photo)

was unsuccessful, service could be discontinued and the line abandoned by Norfolk Southern. From Norfolk Southern's 1987 review of the former NF&D and the Franklin District, it determined that two segments of the line should be abandoned and a third would be a candidate for inclusion in the Thoroughbred Program.

One of the two line segments to be abandoned was a small segment on the western end of the former A&D/NF&D. When the 79.8 mile segment of the NF&D between South Hill, Virginia and Blanche, North Carolina was abandoned as a result of the 1982 merger of the N&W and Southern, a 7.8 mile segment between Blanche and Danville was retained in service and operated by the Southern. In May of 1995, Norfolk Southern decided to abandon

3.10 miles of the line from Blanche (Mile Post 196.9) to East Danville (Mile Post 200), including all of the trackage in the state of North Carolina. Norfolk Southern retained all of the former A&D/NF&D track in Pittsylvania County , Virginia (Mile Post 200 to Mile Post 204.9), which included a one mile section of track past the U. S. Gypsum plant.

A more substantial section of the railroad was abandoned in 1989 following an analysis by Norfolk Southern of the 28.0 mile segment of line in Brunswick and Mecklenburg Counties between Edgerton and South Hill. For purposes of its analysis, Norfolk Southern considered the line in two segments. The first was a seven mile section from Mile Post 89 at Edgerton to Mile Post 96, ap-

Virginia Southern Railroad Extra 512 North crosses the bridge over U. S. RT. 58 at Clarksville on a section of the only remaining trackage of the original A&D line between Clarksville and Jeffress. With its 18-car train on October 21, 1994, GP-40 No. 512, GP-9 No. 618 and GP-40 No. 200 are preparing to return to the tracks of the Southern Railway for the run to Keysville. The Virginia Southern is a division of the North Carolina and Virginia Railroad and is owned by Railtex, the San Antonio, Texas-based holding company of a number of feeder-line railroads. Virginia Southern was created in November of 1988 under the first lease granted by the Norfolk Southern's "Thoroughbred Shortline Program" to operate a 72-mile line from O&H Junction (Oxford), North Carolina to Burkeville, Virginia. (Curt Tillotson, Jr. Photo)

Continuing the A&D's short line tradition in fine fashion, Commonwealth Railway's CF-7 No. 517 rolls out of Suffolk on June 16, 1997 for the 16.5-mile run to West Norfolk. Owned by Rail Link Inc., a subsidiary of Brenco, Inc., the Commonwealth Railroad began operations on August 24, 1989. It purchased the portion of the line from West Norfolk to Churchland and leased the portion from Churchland to Suffolk. As was the case during the operation of the line during both the A&D and NF&D operation, the principal traffic on the line is derived from the chemical plant at West Norfolk. (Russell Underwood Photo)

proximately one mile west of Lawrenceville. The track on this section was 80 or 90 pound rail in fair condition with approximately ten good ties per 39-foot of rail line. The ties were fully plated with two spikes per plate and rail was joined by 24-inch bars with four bolts per bar. The ballast was in good condition and vegetation was under control. There were three fairly large shippers on this section that transported about 1,500 to 1,600 carloads per year.

The next segment of the line was from Mile Post 96 to the line's terminus at Mile Post 117, just west of South Hill. This section had not been maintained as well; however, the structures on the line were in good condition. This section was also laid with 80 to 90 pound rail; however, there were only approximately five good ties per 39-foot of rail line. The ties were fully plated with two spikes per plate and the rail was joined with 24-inch bars with four connecting bolts. However, the ballast on the line was not adequate and vegetation was fairly dense. Significantly, there were only two active shippers (Homecraft, Inc. and Royster, Inc.) located on this segment of the line. Traffic the line had been meager and was declining. Carloads fell from 196 in 1983 to 76 in 1986 and 52 in 1987. Through May of 1988, traffic had consisted of 6 carloads for Homecraft and 17 carloads for Royster. Service between Lawrenceville and South Hill was being provided on an as-needed basis.

On October 15, 1988, Norfolk Southern filed a petition with the Interstate Commerce Commission to abandon the 21.8 miles of line between Mile Post 95.2 at Lawrenceville and Mile Post 117 at the end of the line at South Hill. Permission to abandon the line was granted by the ICC in a decision dated February 3, 1989. The

"official" last run from South Hill (another cleanup trip would be required) occurred on March 15, 1989 and entailed the movement of three freight cars and N&W caboose 555074 behind GP-20 No. 2008. Norfolk Southern Agent-General Yardmaster H. R. Hogan, the Lawrenceville mayor and a newspaper reporter rode the front of the locomotive all the way from South Hill to Lawrenceville on the final run.

The "cleanup trip" to South Hill took place two weeks later. NS GP-20 No. 2008 with N&W caboose 555028 returned on Tuesday night, March 28th to pick up three empty cars that had been left in South Hill. The train crew tied up for the night and, when they departed at 8 a.m. on Wednesday morning for the return trip to Lawrenceville, the history of the rail service to South Hill quietly came to an end. The crew members of the last train to leave South Hill were Engineer R. L. Capps, Conductor J. E. Presson and Brakemen William Moody and Nat Blanton. The abandonment was officially exercised on April 1, 1989 and within a year, the rails had been removed from the line.

While rail service to South Hill came to an end in 1989, the memory of the railroad lives on in the town's former station. The original A&D station at South Hill burned to the ground and was replaced in 1924 with a brick combination freight and passenger station. It was the only brick station ever built on the A&D Railroad. The last passenger train to visit the station was on July 31, 1949 - the date the Southern Railway exited both the passenger business and its lease of the A&D. During its second period of independent operation, the A&D operated the facility as a freight station. The station was finally closed during the period of NF&D

51

operation. Although it had been vacated by the railroad for many years, it had been occupied by other tenants, including a period from 1967 to 1979 when it served as a headquarters for the South Hill Chamber of Commerce.

In May of 1986, the South Hill business community led a successful effort to persuade Norfolk Southern to donate the station to the town. Once the building was formally deeded in 1987 to the South Hill Community Development Association, community leaders launched a renovation campaign. A "Dash for the Depot" fund-raising event garnered over $20,000 in one day. As important as money, about fifty local contractors and workers donated their labor and materials, including replacement of the roof and remodeling of the 1,800-square foot front of the building. On June 10, 1990, a ceremony was held to dedicate the renovated facility. Today, the station's front section (the former waiting room for white passengers) houses the office of the Chamber of Commerce and the former station master's office serves as a conference room. The smaller waiting room (formerly a waiting room for black passengers) now is lined with display cases filled with more than 500 dolls and their accessories, donated to the town by one of its natives, Virginia S. Evans. The larger rear section (the former freight station) now houses the South Hill Model Railroad Museum. Along with a wildlife display, model trains and tracks fill the former freight station. There are also photographs and railroad artifacts, all reminiscent of the early days of railroading in the area.

The centerpiece of the museum is a 60-foot by 12-foot floor space that depicts the A&D Railroad in HO scale. This landscaped model of the A&D was built by Ralph W. Schneider, a master craftsman and lifelong modeler who served as Project Manager for the museum. His family had operated shipworks in their native Germany for centuries and, by the 1980's, Schneider had retired to South Hill after a career as a naval architect. He once used models as a tool for designing boats and gained a reputation for being able to build scale replicas for engineering purposes. As a sideline to his architectural career, Schneider also had formed a model company that was employed by the motion picture industry to create models and special effects for movies. To spruce up the layout, Schneider built the model railroad in three separate eras. The section from the James River to Emporia is the original narrow gauge railroad and depicted life in the 1880's. The track from Emporia to South Hill is fashioned after the Southern Railway era of the 1930's. From South Hill to Danville, the railroad resembles the NF&D of the 1960's. In addition to the models of the trains, Schneider also modeled the landscape and towns along the A&D. Of course, South Hill is the most detailed town on the railroad, with every building and structure surrounding the former station re-created in painstaking detail. While much of the former A&D is now gone, its memory fortunately has been preserved for future generations at the South Hill Model Railroad Museum, a must-see for any fan of the railroad.

The abandonment of the line between Lawrenceville and South Hill also led to the demise of the Lawrenceville freight station. While the Lawrenceville passenger station had been razed in the 1960's, the freight station had served the A&D, NF&D and N&W as a freight agency. The Lawrenceville agency was closed by Norfolk Southern on March 19, 1990 and the work was transferred to the Suffolk agency. In 1991, the Lawrenceville freight station was dismantled, piece by piece, and was salvaged to be used as an addition to a private home located at a ski resort in Banner-Elk, North Carolina. All but the office area of the station was rebuilt at the home to accommodate bedrooms, a playroom and a three-car garage.

While the Norfolk Southern had decided that it should abandon the segments of the former A&D/NF&D between East Danville and Danville and between Lawrenceville and South Hill, it found the 17-mile line between West Norfolk and Suffolk to be a excellent candidate for transfer to a feeder line operator under the provisions of the Thoroughbred Short Line Program. This line, which was still referred to as the West Norfolk Branch, had historically been profitable. However, by 1987, traffic on the branch consisted solely of a low revenue move of stone to Tarmac Lonestar at Boone Siding and shipments to and from the Virginia Chemicals plant at West Norfolk. In 1988, Hoechst Celanese - which had purchased the Virginia Chemicals plant - ceased the movement of sulfur dioxide to and from its plant, resulting in a substantial loss of traffic and revenue to Norfolk Southern. Train service on the branch was being performed not more than three times a week by crews called from the extra board at Suffolk.

The West Norfolk Branch was added to the Thoroughbred Program and Norfolk Southern received bids for the line from two potential operators - Rail Link and Rail Tex. Norfolk Southern considered the bids from these two experienced short line operators and selected Rail Link, Inc., a subsidiary of Brenco, Inc. of Petersburg, Virginia. At that time, Rail Link also owned the Carolina Coastal, which operated a leased short line railroad in Beaufort County, North Carolina. Once its bid was accepted by Norfolk Southern, Rail Link formed a wholly owned subsidiary - the Commonwealth Railway to acquire, operate and lease the line of the West Norfolk Branch as a new rail carrier. Prior to the transfer of the branch to Commonwealth Railway, Hoechst Celanese requested that Norfolk Southern allow it to purchase all of the tracks and right of way of the railroad within the confines of the company's plant at West Norfolk. The railroad agreed and in July of 1989, the chemical company purchased the line of railroad from Mile Post F-0.0 to Mile Post F-0.08.

The transfer of the West Norfolk branch from Norfolk Southern to Commonwealth Railway was accomplished in an agreement between the two railroads dated August 23, 1989. Pursuant to the terms of that agreement, the 3.92 miles of branch in the city of Portsmouth - from the beginning of the branch at Mile Post F-0.08 (West Norfolk) to Mile Post F-4.0 (Churchland) - were sold to the Virginia Commonwealth. The remaining 12.5 miles of track from Churchland to Mile Post F-16.5 (Suffolk) were leased to the short line for a term of 20 years with an option to purchase. From Mile Post F-16. 5 (the beginning of the yard limits at Suffolk), Commonwealth Railway was granted trackage rights to operate over the Norfolk and Western to a junction with the N&W's main line at Mile Post F-17.3 and over the main line to reach the tracks that would be used at Suffolk for interchange between the two railroads.

The last day of Norfolk Southern service on the West Norfolk branch was performed on August 24, 1989. Appropriately, the motive power for the last run of the West Norfolk local was provided by No. 5172, a GP-38-2 diesel which still sported a Southern Railway paint scheme. Currently on the Franklin District, the Suffolk/ Edgerton rock trains are designated as V13/V14. The turnaround local (V31/V32) continues as a Monday through Friday job between Suffolk and Lawrenceville, however, it rarely operates west of Emporia.

CHAPTER 6

THE NARROW GAUGE OPERATIONS - THE CLAREMONT BRANCH

During the two decades following the War Between the States, American railroads began changing the gauge of their tracks to four feet, eight and one-half inches. However, at the same time the established lines were standardizing track gauge, a number of new companies were laying over 5,000 miles of narrow gauge trackage. There was a reason for this surge in building rail lines laid to the narrow measure. They were considerably cheaper to build, equip and maintain than standard gauge lines.

The founders of the A&D were attracted to such economies. The railroad was to be "home owned" and financed with county subscriptions. However, raising money in the South after the war was never an easy task. Moreover, this new railroad was to be built through a rural section of Virginia that had little or no rail service. The county fathers saw the need for a railroad but the citizenry had been less than forward in putting up the money for one.

A narrow gauge line seemed to provide the solution. It would be more economical to construct and operate. Hence, it would be easier to finance. The promoters went to the legislature and came away with a charter to construct a railroad "... the gauge of which shall be three feet ..."

Construction of the A&D commenced in 1883 and soon the little narrow gauge trains were bringing timber out of heavily wooded Surry County to the wharf at Claremont. There connection was made with schooners plying the James River.

The line was barely completed to Emporia in 1885 when the ambitions of the A&D officials expanded and they decided to change the deep water terminal to Norfolk and then build a standard gauge railroad to Danville. The A&D was reincorporated to provide for this change and authority was even granted to "... change the gauge of the road already built ..."

However, the A&D never widened the gauge of the track between Claremont and Emporia. Thereafter, the original 50 miles of the A&D became a narrow gauge branch line of the standard gauge railroad. The A&D and the Southern Railway officially designated the line as the James River Division. It was more commonly known as the "Claremont Branch".

The branch extended from Claremont Wharf on the James River to a connection with the standard gauge main line at James River Junction, a point three and one-half miles east of Emporia. It traversed the Virginia counties of Sussex, Surry and Greenville with 50.42 miles of main track and 3.33 miles of side track.

There were 36 trestles on the line with a total length of 3,573 feet. The largest structure was the three span truss bridge over the Nottoway River just north of Lumberton. It was 20 feet high and contained over 1,000 feet of trestle. Water stations were initially located at Claremont, Savedge and Yale. Later the Savedge water tank was moved to Blackwater. Wooden overtruss turntables with center wheels that were used only for turning narrow gauge locomotives were located at Emporia and Claremont.

There were two significant grades on the branch. Near Waverly the line rose from the Assamoosic Swamp to the top of a hill known as Birdsong. Northbound trains of more than 15 cars had to double the hill at Birdsong. A siding was located at the foot of the hill for trains to set off cars. Southbound trains encountered a grade of 3 to 3-1/2 per cent when pulling up from Claremont Wharf to the town of Claremont.

The branch was crossed at grade by the Virginian Railway at Ward, approximately 10 miles northeast of James River Junction, by the Norfolk and Western Railway at Waverly and by the Atlantic Coast Line Railroad at Emporia. It was also crossed by the West Hope Branch of the Surry, Sussex and Southampton Railway between Lumberton and Yale at a point called Griffin Station.

The branch connected with the main line of the A&D at James River Junction, but there was practically no interchange of traffic with the main line. The traffic on the branch was almost exclusively lumber and cordwood which was transported by the boat lines operating from Claremont Wharf.

In 1889 a narrow gauge branch line of 5 miles was built off of the Claremont Branch from Savedge to Alcott's Mill. However, this line was simply a saw mill siding. When the mill closed in 1896 the

In a rare photograph that was probably taken around 1900, the train and engine crew pose with their narrow gauge train at Claremont. The locomotive is Southern Railway 4-6-0 No. N5 (formerly A&D No. 5) that was built by Baldwin Locomotive Works in 1886 and passed to the Southern under its lease of the A&D in 1899. Note that the locomotive is still equipped with a link and pin coupler and the original lamp headlight. (Russell Wayne Davis Collection)

Throughout the period of the Southern's lease of the A&D, one mixed train was operated in each direction over the Claremont Branch daily except Sunday. Train No. 103, shown here with 4-6-0 No. N6, is departing Claremont for its 54-mile afternoon run to Emporia. (J. W. Browder, Jr. Collection)

tracks were taken up from the Savedge Branch.

Stations were located at Grizzard, Masons, Hilda, Yale, Lumberton, Homeville, Waverly, Savedge, Spring Grove and Claremont. They were frame buildings, board and batton, with a tin shingle roof.

At Claremont Wharf there was a combination freight and passenger depot, a one story warehouse on a wharf and three other wharves that extended into the river. Together, the four wharves could accommodate seven schooners.

The town of Claremont was located about one mile south of Claremont Wharf. At Claremont there was another combination freight and passenger station, an engine house with two tracks running through it, an oil house, sand house and a 50-foot turntable.

The branch joined the A&D's main line at James River Junction. From that point to Emporia the main line was equipped with a third rail for a distance of 3.79 miles to accommodate trains of either standard or narrow gauge. The third rail also crossed through the A&D's crossing at grade with the double track main line of the Atlantic Coast Line Railroad at Emporia. One-tenth of a mile of

side track at Emporia was equipped with third rail. In addition, there were 12 side tracks at Emporia equipped for narrow gauge operation.

The narrow gauge service and repair facilities were located at Emporia. A frame seven stall engine house and wooden 52-foot turntable were located opposite the standard gauge station near the corner of Main and Atlantic streets. This old engine house served as the repair shop for all narrow gauge equipment. For major repairs the locomotives were loaded on flat cars equipped with rails and were sent to the Lawrenceville shops.

All of the A&D's narrow gauge equipment passed to the Southern Railway under the lease of August 31, 1899. An inventory of A&D equipment taken prior to the lease listed the steam locomotives as 2-6-0 No. 2 and 4-6-0's Nos. 5 and 6. Nos. 2 and 5 were purchased new by the A&D in 1886. No. 6 was acquired from the Talledega and Coosa Valley Railroad. The A&D's narrow gauge rolling stock consisted of 15 box cars, 80 flat cars, 1 combination car and 4 caboose/camp cars.

After the lease of the A&D, the locomotives were renumbered to become Southern N-2, N-5 and N-6. In addition, the Southern supplemented the Claremont Branch's locomotive roster with the N-3, a former Elberton Air Line 4-6-0 that had been built by Baldwin in 1878.

As was characteristic of all narrow gauge operations, rail service on the Claremont Branch was conducted on a leisurely schedule. The only scheduled run was a mixed passenger and freight train that operated daily except Sunday. Train No. 104 left Emporia around 7 o'clock in the morning and arrived at Claremont before noon. Train No. 103 departed Claremont Wharf at 1:00 p.m. and was scheduled to make the 54-mile run back to Emporia by 5:00 p.m.

During the final years of

In a classic photograph, Train No. 104 with 4-6-0 No. N6 is shown upon arrival at Claremont Wharf in summer of 1910. This train departed Emporia at 7 a.m. and reached Claremont around noon, with scheduled stops at James River Junction, Gray, Yale, Homeville, Waverly and Spring Grove. Note the last car, which is a combination baggage and RPO car. (Shelby F. Lowe Collection)

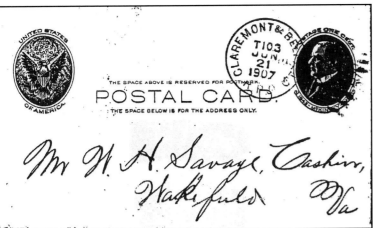

narrow gauge operation, service was reduced to one tri-weekly mixed train. This train ran from Emporia to Claremont on Mondays, Wednesdays and Fridays, and from Claremont to Emporia on Tuesdays, Thursdays and Saturdays. In addition to performing what little work there was on the branch, the crew also did most of the switching work at Emporia.

There were no industries in the territory served by the branch other than the Gray Lumber Company at Waverly and the Co-Operative Creamery at Spring Grove. The Gray Lumber Company shipped almost entirely via the Norfolk and Western Railway because the N&W could place standard gauge cars for loading while shipment over the branch necessitated transfer of all lading at Emporia to standard gauge cars from the narrow gauge. Other than peanuts which could be shipped, but which were trucked, and butter from the Creamery, which was also handled by trucks, there was nothing to produce tonnage on the branch other than forest products.

Forest products always constituted approximately seventy-five per cent of the traffic on the Claremont Branch. In the early years of operation, a large proportion of the lumber produced along the branch moved to Claremont Wharf for trans-shipment by vessel principally to Baltimore, Philadelphia and New York. However, by the 1920's most of the timber in the territory served by the branch had been cut over at least once and there was very little large timber left. Depletion of the timber resulted in a progressive decline in traffic on the branch.

This business was further reduced in the late 1920's when regular boat service from Claremont Wharf was ended. With the movements by Claremont Wharf eliminated, all remaining traffic had to move through Emporia. This required the costly and burdensome transfer between narrow gauge and standard gauge which had to be absorbed by the Southern to meet the competition with the route via Waverly and the N&W.

By February of 1932 traffic had declined to the point that there were no carload shipments to the branch and only four from the branch. On September 9, 1932, the Southern made application to the Inter-

state Commerce Commission for authority to abandon operations. Since the Southern Railway did not own the branch, it had no standing to petition the ICC for abandonment of the line. It could only ask for the authority to discontinue operations thereon. The ICC granted the Southern's petition in an order dated November 4, 1932. Operation of trains on the branch by Southern ceased thirty days later on December 5th.

The third rail was removed from the main line between James River Junction and Emporia as well as from the side tracks in Emporia in March of 1933. Following removal of the third rail, connection was broken at James River Junction and the narrow gauge trackage was removed for a clearance distance from the main line.

All of the narrow gauge locomotives and rolling stock were loaded on standard gauge flat cars and were taken to Lawrenceville pending disposition. A third rail was laid on a 270-foot long shop yard track at Lawrenceville for storage of the narrow gauge locomotives.

At the end, the branch had three locomotives (Nos. N-2, N-5 and N-6) and 117 pieces of rolling stock. The rolling stock included 3 passenger cars, 24 boxcars, 81 flat cars, 5 work equipment cars and a caboose (No. X-32). There were also 6 motor cars. The 4-6-0 No. N-3 did not last to see the abandonment. It had been scrapped in Lawrenceville in 1929. All of the remaining narrow gauge locomotives and rolling stock were sent to Southern's shops at Spencer, North Carolina and were scrapped in the spring of 1934.

However, even though the operation of trains by the Southern Railway came to an end, logging trains continued to be operated on the Claremont Branch by the Gray Lumber Company of Waverly. For a number of years this lumber company had been party to a working agreement with Southern for use of the track south of Waverly. Under the agreement, Gray paid the Southern $20.00 a day for each day that the company's log trains operated over the branch. Prior to 1932, Gray Lumber Company operated log trains one or two days a week on the branch as far south as Grizzard to bring logs to the sawmill at Waverly.

To assure the preservation of logging rights on the branch after the Southern abandoned operations, the lumber company en-

This scheduled service for Southern Railway mixed trains between Claremont Wharf and Emporia changed very little during its operation of the branch between 1899 and 1932. This schedule is from the Southern Railway's public timetable for June 27, 1926. (William E. Griffin, Jr. Collection)

TABLE 24		CLAREMONT WHARF AND EMPORIA (Norfolk Division.)						
	Mixed 103 Ex Sun	Miles	Eastern Time (Narrow Gauge)		Mixed 104 Ex Sun			
	PM		Lv	Ar	AM			
	12 20	.0	CLAREMONT WHARF .Va.		11 45			
	12 30	1.2	Claremont................	"	11 30			
	12 42	5.8	Spring Grove............	"	11 05			
	f12 52	9.2	Savedge.................	"	f10 50			
	1 30	17.3	Waverly.................	"	10 20			
	1 55	25.2	Homeville...............	"	8 50			
	f	27.9	Burt....................	"	f			
	f 2 10	30.5	Lumberton...............	"	f 8 30			
	2 30	35.4	Yale....................	"	8 10			
	f 2 45	38.4	Hilda...................	"	f 8 00			
	3 00	40.7	Gray....................	"	7 50			
	f 3 15	43.8	Masons..................	"	f 7 35			
	f 3 30	47.8	Grizzard................	"	f 7 20			
	3 40	50.4	James River Jct.........	"	7 10			
	4 00	54.1	EMPORIA.................	"	7 00			
	PM		Ar	Lv	AM			

55

Steamboat service on the James River between Richmond and Norfolk was conducted by the Powhatan Steamboat Company, that had been founded in 1845 as an affiliate of the Baltimore Steam Packet Company. In a photograph taken circa 1895, the steamship "Pocahontas" of the Powhatan Steamboat Company is shown on the James River at Richmond. (William E. Griffin, Jr. Collection)

lease on the southern section of the branch.

On August 11, 1938, the A&D joined with the Southern in an application to the ICC to completely abandon the Claremont Branch. On October 18, 1938 the ICC issued a certificate permitting the abandonment of the line effective November 20, 1938. Thereafter, the Southern sold the branch for the account of the A&D and dismantled the line from James River Junction to Claremont Wharf.

Only one small section of the branch was not dismantled. The Gray Lumber Company purchased a short strip of the narrow gauge main line adjacent to their plant in Waverly. This trackage was located between the town and the Norfolk and Western Railway's crossing at grade with the branch near the present North Street crossing.

Today, almost 70 years after the abandonment, little remains to show that there was ever a narrow gauge railroad between Emporia and Claremont Wharf. Some of the old depots such as Claremont, Homeville, Lumberton and Grizzard still stand as farm buildings. However, most of the little hamlets that existed along the branch have vanished. The bridge timbers can still be seen in Assamoosic Swamp as can a portion of the former right of way between Waverly and Homeville. But the rest is gone. Nature has reclaimed the A&D's Claremont Branch.

tered into a new lease with the railroad in November of 1932. Under this lease, the Southern agreed to continue the logging contract with Gray and even extended the logging company's rights to provide for operation over the entire Claremont Branch. Gray agreed to assume the maintenance of the branch for its own operating purposes.

The lease divided the branch into two sections approximately at Waverly and gave the lumber company the option to give up maintenance and operation of that portion between Waverly and Claremont Wharf. This the lumber company did in the fall of 1933. In June of 1938 the lumber company also cancelled its

The steamship "Pocahontas" is docked at the Claremont Wharf depot awaiting arrival of the mixed train from Emporia. (William E. Griffin, Jr. Collection)

Southern Railway mixed train No. 104, with 4-6-0 No. N5, rolls through Spring Grove approaching the grade crossing with Route 10. The buildings in the background are the Rogers' Store and the old post office. This rare photograph of a narrow gauge train in operation was taken in 1921. (Jack Huber Collection)

In another rare photograph, a Southern Railway maintenance crew takes some time off from their pile driving duties to pose on a trestle with their work train. The train and crew were photographed at an unidentified location (there were 36 trestles on the 54-mile branch between Claremont Wharf and Emporia). The locomotive and the wooden Southern Railway boxcar behind the engine are also unidentified. However, the narrow gauge flat car behind the boxcar is No. 49252 and Pile Driver No. 32 is mounted on flat car No. 49272. Behind the pile driver, and providing coal for the operation by its steam engine, is the tender from steam locomotive No. 3892 that has been mounted on another narrow gauge flat car. The 3892 was the former A&D standard gauge 4-4-0 steam locomotive No. 25. When this locomotive passed to the Southern under its lease of the A&D, the locomotive was renumbered 3892 in 1907. The locomotive was scrapped in 1914, but its tender was retained and converted to work train service. (August A. Thieme Collection)

ATLANTIC AND DANVILLE RAILWAY
NARROW GAUGE STEAM LOCOMOTIVES

Roster of A&D/Southern Railway narrow gauge steam locomotives.

A&D NUMBER	SOU NUMBER	TYPE	CYLINDERS	BUILDER	DATE	DISPOSITION
2	N-2	2-6-0	14 × 18	Rhode Island	1886	Scrapped, Spencer, 1934
	N-3	4-6-0	12 × 16	Baldwin	1878	Scrapped, Lawrenceville 1929
5	N-5	4-6-0	14 × 20	Baldwin	1886	Scrapped, Spencer, 1934
6	N-6	4-6-0	14 × 20	Baldwin	1888	Scrapped, Spencer, 1934

NOTES:

(1) N-3 was ex-Southern N-805 and ex-Elberton Air Line #1.

Three former A&D narrow gauge locomotives - the 2, 5 and 6 - passed to the Southern Railway under the lease. A&D 2-6-0 No. 2, renumbered the N2 by the Southern, was built by the Rhode Island Locomotive Works in 1886. This photograph of the N2 was taken at Emporia in August of 1932. (H. T. Crittenden Photo/C. K. Marsh, Jr. Collection)

With the bell ringing to herald its approach, Southern 4-6-0 N5 (former A&D No. 5) brings its train in
Emporia in 1932. Note the dual gauge trackag
that was used between James River Junction ar
Emporia to permit the operation of both narrow ar
standard gauge trains. The N-5's boiler was rebu
at Southern Railway's Spencer Shops in 1927. Th
firebox was extended one foot and boiler pressu
was increased from 130-lbs. to 175-lbs. The sh
also put a bigger steam dome on the locomotive (
seen in this photo) and increased the engine weig
by 1300-lbs. Birdsong Hill was the ruling grade o
the Claremont Branch. Prior to its rebuild, the N
could only handle 6 to 9 loads over the hill. Aft
its boiler was rebuilt, it could handle 15 cars ov
Birdsong Hill. (C. K. Marsh, Jr. Collection)

In an early view of Southern 4-6-0 N5, the locomotive is
shown crossing at grade the main line tracks of the Norfolk and Western Railroad at Waverly in March of 1917.
This locomotive was built by Baldwin Locomotive Works
in 1886 and was scrapped at Spencer, North Carolina
in 1934. (Karl E. Schlachter Photo/H. K. Vollrath Collection)

Southern Railway 4-6-0 No. N6 was built for the A&D
Baldwin Locomotive Works in 1888. It was photograph
at Emporia on September 17, 1932 in another view th
clearly shows the dual narrow and standard gauge trac
age at that terminal. (Mallory Hope Ferrell Collection)

Locomotive Engineer T. H. Braswell and his crew
pose with the N6 in a photograph taken at Waverly in
1911. (Shelby F. Lowe Collection)

Spring Grove was the first station stop north of Claremont Wharf and was located at the intersection of State Routes 40 and 10. The small community had a post office, general store and the railroad depot. The depot was a frame building with a shingle roof, 18-feet X 26-feet, and was used for both passengers and freight. This photograph of the station was taken circa 1920's. (Jack Huber Collection)

The Grizzard depot, shown in this 1917 photograph, was almost identical to the station at Yale. The Grizzard station was also battened, with a tin shingled roof and measured 20-feet X 42-feet. Interestingly, the Grizzard depot also has been preserved and today serves as a farm storage building. (William E. Griffin, Jr. Collection)

This circa 1920's photograph of the Yale depot clearly shows the two-tone paint scheme applied to all stations on the Claremont Branch. Note also the old style signboard that reads "James River Junction 14.9 Miles" and "Claremont Wharf 5.6 Miles". The men in front of the station were apparently strong union members. The man to the left is holding a Southern Railway train bulletin board on which has been written "Solid ORT", which meant they were strong members of the "Order of Railroad Telegraphers". Perhaps a representational election was underway at the time. The Yale depot was battened, with a tin shingled roof and measured 20-feet X 42-feet. This building still exists today. It was purchased and moved to a nearby farm where its owner uses it for storage. (Jack Huber Collection)

By 1932, the Southern Railway fleet of Claremont Branch narrow gauge passenger equipment consisted of three cars. Nos. 2 and 5 were coaches and No. 6 was a combination car that accommodated passengers, baggage and the Railway Post Office. All were wood side, truss rod cars. Two of these cars - coach No. 5 and combination car No. 6 - bring up the rear of Train No. 103 as it arrives at Emporia in 1932. (H. T. Crittenden Photo)

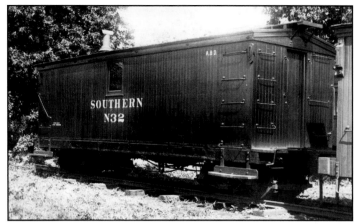

The N32, shown here at Emporia, was the only caboose car operate over the Claremont Branch. The car was stenciled to indicate A&D owne ship of this piece of rolling stock. (H. T. Crittenden Photo)

Southern Railway narrow gauge Tool Car No. T-264 was photographed at Emporia alongside two of the wooden passenger coaches. (H. T. Crittenden Photo)

When the operation of the Claremont Bran was abandoned in 1934, the Southern Railwa was operating 24 narrow gauge boxcars ov the line. Boxcar No. 104, shown here at Emp ria in 1932, was formerly A&D No. 104, one the original pieces of rolling stock turned ov to the Southern Railway when it leased t A&D in 1899. (H. T. Crittenden Photo)

Due to the nature of the freight traffic handled over the branch (forest products), the most prominent piece of rolling stock was the flat car. When the Southern Railway leased the A&D in 1899, the A&D turned over 301 flat cars to the Southern. When the branch was abandoned in 1934, the Southern Railway was still operating 81 such cars. Southern Railway narrow gauge flat car No. 16 was formerly A&D No. 16, another piece of the 1899 original rolling stock. Here it is shown at Emporia in 1932. In the background is Southern Railway narrow gauge box car No. 3736. (H. T. Crittenden Photo)

CHAPTER 7

THE A&D NAVY -
NORFOLK HARBOR OPERATIONS

Cotton was almost unknown at the port of Norfolk during the antebellum period. However, that situation changed quickly with the conclusion of the War Between the States.

Norfolk's two railroads - the Norfolk and Petersburg (a predecessor of the Norfolk and Western) and the Seaboard and Roanoke (a predecessor of the Seaboard Air Line) - established connections in 1866 with railroads in the cotton states. Within two years these railroads were pouring cotton into Norfolk.

Bales of cotton were seen at every turn and city newspapers boasted that Norfolk would soon be the nation's greatest cotton port. Their pride was not without foundation. At that time, Norfolk was receiving more cotton than either Charleston or Savannah.

Much of the Southern cotton was brought to Norfolk for export. A cotton exchange was organized

Following its entry into the Norfolk area in the 1890's, the Southern Railway built a substantial terminal at Pinners Point on the Portsmouth side of the Elizabeth River. To bridge the mile and a quarter of river between its freight houses at Norfolk and Pinners Point, the Southern conducted a naval operation consisting of a tugboat, an open barge, four car floats, fourteen house barges and a floating pile driver. This aerial view of the Pinners Point terminal, taken in 1959, shows the Southern Railway rail yard and piers to the left; and, the rail yard and piers of the Atlantic Coast Line Railroad to the right. Southern Railway freight and passenger operations over the A&D were handled through the Pinners Point terminal during the 50-year lease. When the A&D resumed independent operation in 1949, it was granted use of the ACL's Pinners Point pier and yard facilities where it could directly interchange with both the Southern and the ACL. To reach the terminal facilities, the A&D was granted trackage rights over the ACL from Boone to Pinners Point. (Tal Carey Collection)

in 1874 and the establishment of two compress houses made possible foreign shipments directly from Norfolk's wharves. With white clouds of escaping steam and the deafening noise that accompanied them, the steam-driven compresses reduced the bales of cotton to a more compact size so as to take up less space in a ship's hold.

One of the early compress operators was the Seaboard Cotton Press Company, owned by the Bain family, with compresses in both Norfolk and Portsmouth. It was on the Seaboard Cotton Press Company's Portsmouth

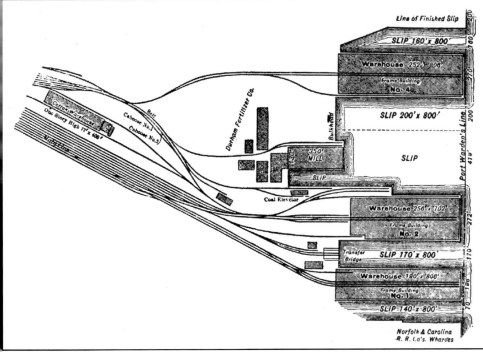

This 1890's diagram of the Pinners Point terminal shows the rail trackage to the wharehouses and piers then operated by the Southern Railway (top) and the ACL predecessor company, the Norfolk and Carolina Railroad (below). When the Southern Railway leased the A&D in 1899, it closed the A&D's own deep water terminal at West Norfolk and moved all operations to the Pinners Point facility. (William E. Griffin, Jr. Collection)

The Southern Railway's navy at Norfolk was comprised of a fleet of house barges, car floats and two tugboats, the "Memphis" and the "Louisville". Both tugs had been owned by the A&D and passed to the Southern in 1899 under the provisions of the 50-year lease. The Southern purchased both tugs from the A&D in 1946. The "Louisville", formerly known as the A&D's "Thomas A. Bain", was 83-feet long, 19-feet wide, weighed 87 tons and drew 9 feet of water. Shown in this 1948 photo at Pinners Point, the "Louisville" was primarily assigned by the Southern to tow house barges and car floats across the Elizabeth River. (H. Reid Photo)

property that the A&D established its first deep water terminal on the Elizabeth River.

The British investors financed the construction of the A&D's main line because they were also interested in the exportation of cotton. In 1888, over 230,000 bales were exported from the ports at Norfolk and Portsmouth to Great Britain. The A&D was viewed as a potential pipeline to ship cotton from the deep South. These same British investors even gained control of the Seaboard Cotton Press Company. Unfortunately, the expected boom in cotton traffic never occurred on the A&D and by 1894 cotton represented only 2% of the railroad's total freight tonnage.

The A&D's deep water terminal at Portsmouth had been established in 1887. Two years later, the company opened another deep water terminal at West Norfolk on the Western Branch of the Elizabeth River. The railroad operated both facilities until 1894 when it withdrew from Portsmouth in favor of the West Norfolk site.

It was during this period that the A&D acquired its fleet of "floating equipment". Initially, all of the vessels operated by the A&D were registered in the name of its subsidiary, the Seaboard Cotton Press Company and were leased back to the railroad. The A&D purchased all of them in 1893.

The first ship to serve the A&D was the "Thomas A. Bain", an 83-foot iron hull steam-powered tugboat. It was built at Philadelphia in 1883 for the Seaboard Cotton Press Company. The "Bain" was also used for general towing service as were two other A&D steam-powered tugs, the "F. A. Low" and the "Virginia".

When the A&D opened its new West Norfolk terminal in 1889, the Seaboard Cotton Press Company acquired two steam-powered passenger boats. Both were used to ferry passengers, mail, baggage and express across the Elizabeth River to Norfolk.

The 139-foot side-paddle "River Belle" was built in 1846 at New York and had been used for a number of years to transport passengers across Long Island Sound on the Hudson River. It served the A&D for only a short period for when it was determined that the railroad's passenger business did not require the two boats, the "River Belle" was sold in 1893.

The other steamboat acquired in 1889 was the "City of Chester". This 109-foot steamer with a hull of Maine timber had been commissioned in 1872 for service on the Delaware River for the Philadelphia and Chester Transportation Company. When purchased by the Seaboard Cotton Press Company it was being operated by the Erie Railroad in New York harbor.

The A&D also owned four barges, a car float, one yawl and one floating pile driver. Two the barges were covered and two were open. The A&D car float named "Dispatch", which was out of service by 1890, was used to transport freight cars from Norfolk to the Cape Charles connection with the New York, Philadelphia and Norfolk Railroad (a predecessor of the Pennsylvania Railroad).

All of this floating equipment passed to the Southern Railway in 1899 when it entered into its 50-year lease of the A&D. The Southern promptly changed the names of both the "Thomas A. Bain" and the "City of Chester". The "Bain" became the "Louisville" and the "Chester" was renamed the "Memphis". The "Memphis" was rebuilt with a more powerful engine so it could perform combination passenger-tugboat service. The Southern also equipped the "Louisville" with passenger accommodations so it could be used for that duty when the "Memphis" was out of service.

These two A&D vessels spend most of their career working for the Southern Railway. When the Southern assumed operations

The Southern Railway's tugboat "Memphis" (formerly the A&D's "City of Chester" was 109-feet long, 22-feet wide, weighed 177 tons and drew 8 feet of water. Until July 19, 1948, when she made her last passenger run, the "Memphis" was assigned to ferry Southern Railway passengers between downtown Norfolk and Pinners Point, where the railway's line to Norfolk ended. In this photograph, taken on the morning of October 2, 1947, the "Memphis" is shown alongside Southern Railway Train No. 4, that has just arrived at Pinners Point following its overnight run from Danville. (Courtesy of the Mariner's Museum; Newport News, Va.)

under the lease in 1899, it abolished the Norfolk and West Norfolk agencies of the A&D and passed all A&D traffic through the Southern's Norfolk and Pinners Point terminals.

The Pinners Point terminal, opened in 1895, was the hub of Southern's freight operations in the Norfolk area. Switch crews made up the outbound trains and sorted the inbound freight cars according to destination. Much of their work involved separating freight cars that contained carload shipments from those that contained less-than-carload (L.C.L.) shipments.

The L.C.L. shipments were transported in house barges across the mile and a quarter stretch of the Elizabeth River that separated Pinners Point and Norfolk. Painted bright red, the house barges looked like floating freight houses and were towed across the river by tugboats.

Most of the carload freight shipments were interchanged with the Norfolk and Portsmouth Belt Line Railway for delivery to industries. However, carload traffic destined for waterfront industries not served by the Belt Line was handled across the river on car floats.

The car float was an open barge with railroad tracks on its deck. Freight cars were moved from the tracks on shore onto the car float by means of a floating bridge which had mating sections of track arranged to rise and fall with the tide. A yard engine with three empty cars attached would push the cars across the floating bridge onto the car float. The purpose of the three empty cars between the engine and the cars was to keep the weight of the heavy locomotive off the floating bridge.

The largest of the Southern's car floats had a capacity of eight

freight cars. The smallest was capable of transporting four cars. The car floats were maneuvered across the river by tugboat and then moored beside warehouses along the river front. The freight cars never left the car floats on the Norfolk side and were either reloaded by the shipper or returned empty to Pinners Point terminal for reloading.

The maroon and yellow trim steamboat "Memphis" was assigned to ferry the patrons of the Southern's passenger trains between the end of the rail line at Pinners Point and the wharf at the foot of Jackson Street in downtown Norfolk. After making the assigned passenger trips, the "Memphis" often assisted the "Louisville" in towing car floats and house barges across the river.

The Southern purchased both the "Memphis" and the "Louisville" from the A&D in 1946. The "Memphis" made its last passenger run the night of July 19, 1948, but it was retained by the Southern and assumed the tugboat assignments when the "Louisville's" steam engine was replaced with a new diesel engine in 1951. The "Memphis" was never converted to diesel power and was finally sold for scrap after 80 years of service in 1952. The Southern sold the "Louisville" to the W. T. Coppedge and Son Company of Jacksonville, Florida in 1963.

The A&D had no harbor facilities of its own when it resumed independent operations in 1949. Having sold its floating equipment to the Southern and with its former West Norfolk piers practically non-existent, the A&D's traffic for the Norfolk area had to be handled through interchange with the Norfolk and Portsmouth Belt Line Railway via the trackage rights over the Atlantic Coast Line Railroad.

Pinners Point served as the make-up and break-up point for Southern Railway trains serving the Norfolk area. Cars were separated according to destination of the freight and whether it was carload or less-than-carload freight. Most of the Southern's river traffic at Norfolk involved less-than-carload freight and was moved between Norfolk and Pinners Point by house barges and tugboats. Here the "Memphis" is shown maneuvering a barge on the Elizabeth River. (Southern Railway Photo)

Some carload freight crossed the river on car floats going to and from waterfront industries that were not served by the Norfolk and Portsmouth Belt Line Railway. Between the freight house piers, tracks ran to the water's edge where a floating bridge was used so cars could be moved directly onto car floats. The car floats were then maneuvered across the river by tugboat and were moored beside the warehouses along the river front where the contents of the cars could be unloaded, the cars never leaving the car floats. Here the "Memphis" is shown alongside a car float that has been moored at an industry for unloading. (Southern Railway Photo)

CHAPTER 8

WEST NORFOLK TO DANVILLE -
STATIONS AND STRUCTURES

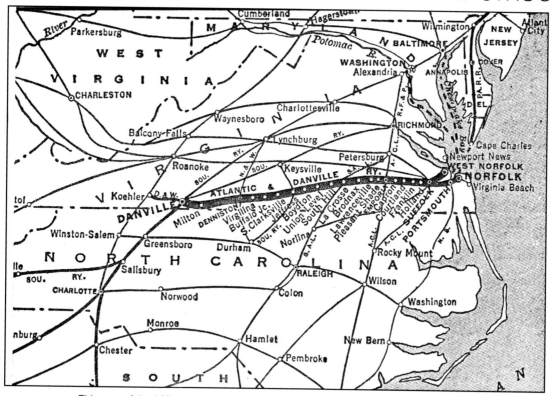

This map of the A&D and its connections shows the principal stations along the line.

The West Norfolk station was built in 1896 to serve as a ferry passenger station for the A&D's waterfront on the Elizabeth River. When a major portion of the A&D's West Norfolk terminal facility was leased to the Virginia Smelting Company (the first chemical company at that location), railroad workmen greased the rails, hooked a locomotive to the station and pulled it up the tracks to a new location a few hundred yards west of the chemical facility. From that location at 3400 West Norfolk Road, the station served the Southern, A&D and NF&D until the freight agency was closed in 1982. This view of the station was taken in 1948. (William E. Griffin, Jr. Collection)

The A&D's line between West Norfolk and Suffolk crossed at grade the ACL's line between Rocky Mount, via Suffolk, and Pinners Point at Boone. The A&D constructed its rail crossing over the track of the ACL's predecessor West Branch Railway Company in 1888. Subsequently, an interlocking plant was constructed at that location. This photograph of the Boone interlocking tower was taken on January 10, 1959. (H. Reid Photo)

This view of the Boone interlocking was taken in 1948 looking towards Drivers and Suffolk on the ACL line from Pinners Point. The A&D's West Norfolk line to Suffolk crosses from left to right. The connecting track between the two lines is to the left in the photograph. At Boone, derails were located on the A&D main line on each side of the ACL controlled by a three lever ground throw arrangement that was electrically locked. The route was normally set for the ACL, with trains restricted to 20 miles per hour and required to stop short of the home signal if in the stop position. A&D trains stopped at the crossing clear of the home signals and a member of the train crew, if there was no approaching ACL train, threw the derails and set the route for the A&D train. The interlocking was removed from Boone in 1963 and gates were installed at that location at the expense of the NF&D. (William E. Griffin, Jr. Collection)

The tracks of six railroads - the A&D, N&W, Virginian, SAL, Norfolk Southern and ACL - passed through Suffolk enroute to the port of Norfolk. Commonly known as "the peanut center of the world", Suffolk played an important role in the freight operations of the independently operated A&D and the N&W-controlled NF&D. This early view of the A&D's station at Suffolk was taken on July 26, 1917 and shows the two-tone paint scheme the railroad applied to its buildings. (William E. Griffin, Jr. Collection)

This 1948 view at the Suffolk Tower shows the A&D line from West Norfolk in the foreground as it crosses the double track main line of the N&W. To the right is the connecting track from the A&D line to the N&W Suffolk passenger station with that station's platforms visible in the distance. Beginning in 1912, the Southern Railway passenger trains between Norfolk and Danville used the so-called Union Passenger facilities of the N&W at Suffolk. Operation into the N&W station required the Southern trains to make a back-up movement to return to their line. The interlocking tower at Suffolk was not owned by the N&W. It was built on N&W property at the joint expense of the Southern, ACL and Norfolk Southern to afford the crossing of the N&W by the trains of those railroads. (William E. Griffin, Jr. Collection)

Southern Railway Ks-class 2-8-0 No. 739 drifts across Washington Street in Suffolk on June 11, 1949. Immediately to the right in the photo is the ACL's Suffolk passenger station. Just ahead and across Washington Street, is the A&D/Southern's freight station. (H. Reid Photo)

Located at Mile Post 29, 12 miles west of Suffolk, the combination freight and passenger station at Holland was typical of the stations designed by the Southern Railway. The station was built by the Southern in 1905. (William E. Griffin, Jr. Collection)

Franklin was one of the busiest freight stations. Here, the A&D interchanged with the SAL Railway and served a number of local industries. Located on the A&D were two large peanut processing plants, a large paper mill and several smaller paper mills and industries. In addition to the passenger station, there was a separate freight station, section tool house and water tank for steam locomotives, all seen in this view looking east in 1948. (William E. Griffin, Jr. Collection)

Westbound A&D Train No. 69, behind RS-2's Nos. 103 and 105, passes the Franklin station on March 10, 1959. (Mallory Hope Ferrell Photo)

The wooden A&D station at Franklin was torn down in June of 1963. It was replaced in December of that year by the NF&D with a new combination freight station and office building. This building, shown here on August 27, 1982, was build by Kingsberry Homes, a new shipper that had just located on the NF&D at Emporia and was a modified version of one of the manufactured homes built by that industry. It would be the only new station build by the NF&D. (William E. Griffin, Jr. Photo)

A light snow covers the ground at Courtland as we look west down the A&D main line in 1948. The small building beside the passenger depot is the baggage room. West of the passenger depot on the other side of Main Street is the freight station. That's the passing track to the right of the main line and a side track came off the main line and passed behind both the freight and passenger stations. (William E. Griffin, Jr. Collection)

A&D Agent Graham Atkins poses outside the Pope station in a photograph taken circa-1920's. The station was closed during the Depression years of the 1930's. (J. W. Browder, Jr. Collection)

This view of the Capron station looking east in 1948, gives a good view of the freight portion of the combination station and the platform around that section of the building. A signalman is working on the station's semaphore signal. (William E. Griffin, Jr. Collection)

Located at Mile Post 60, the Drewryville combination passenger and freight station was built by the Southern Railway in 1907. Like all stations built in the South during that period, it had separate entrances for "White" and "Colored" patrons. The train board which listed the arrival and departure times of trains is located to the left of the "White" entrance. (William E. Griffin, Jr. Collection)

Emporia was another important station on the A&D. At Emporia, the A&D interchanged traffic with the ACL's Richmond to Jacksonville line and the main lines of the two railroads crossed at grade. A narrow gauge branch line was operated from Emporia to Claremont and a standard gauge branch line ran from Emporia to the Hitchcock lumber mill. The Emporia station, shown here in a September, 1967 photo, was located on the corner of Main and Atlantic Streets, opposite the yard and six-stall roundhouse and turntable of the old narrow gauge branch. (John F. Gilbert Photo)

This substantial two-story combination freight and passenger station was built by the A&D at Edgerton in 1889, where the builders of the A&D had intended to construct their railroad shops. However, when they had difficulty purchasing land from the local residents at Edgerton, the railroad pushed the line west to Lawrenceville and established their terminal and shop facility. This photograph of the Edgerton station was taken on July 30, 1917. (William E. Griffin, Jr. Collection)

The small combination freight and passenger station that had been built by the A&D in 1888 at Pleasant Shade had been gone for many years when this photo of the passenger shed at that location was taken in 1948. (William E. Griffin, Jr. Collection)

The Southern Railway replaced the A&D's two-story station at Edgerton with this neat, but smaller frame station. This photograph of the Edgerton station was taken in 1948. (William E. Griffin, Jr. Collection)

Lawrenceville was located at approximately the middle of the line between Norfolk and Danville. Construction of the railroad reached Lawrenceville on August 15, 1889 and it was selected as the site for the railroad's shops and division headquarters. This is a 1948 view from the Hicks Street overpass looking west at the Lawrenceville facilities. To the right is the two-story passenger station/division headquarters building. To the left is the freight station. In the distance, behind the freight station, are the Lawrenceville shops and straight ahead is the yard and water tank for steam locomotives. (William E. Griffin, Jr. Collection)

This photo of the Lawrenceville station was taken in 1948. The building was built by the A&D in 1899 prior to the lease of the railroad to the Southern Railway. The first floor served as the passenger station. The second floor provides offices for the division headquarters and train dispatcher. The wood frame drop siding building had a tin shingle roof and a porch that extended the width of the front of the building. (William E. Griffin, Jr. Collection)

Looking east at Lawrenceville in 1958 with the passenger station on the left and freight station on the right. A boxcar has been spotted at the freight station for loading. Built in 1900, the freight station was also a wood frame building with a tin singled roof. An elevated platform extended from the agent's office beyond the length of the building and enabled freight to be handled directly to and from the cars and the station. (William E. Griffin, Jr. Photo)

This diagram shows the location of the various facilities at the Lawrenceville terminal. (William E. Griffin, Jr. Collection)

Two depots, one for passengers and another for freight, was well as a storehouse, car shops, coach shed, tin shop, carpentry shop, blacksmith shop, machine shop, eight-stall roundhouse and turntable were located at Lawrenceville. They are all visible in this 1945 aerial view of the Lawrenceville. (William E. Griffin, Jr. Collection)

Brodnax was located at Mile Post 107, on the boundary of Brunswick and Mecklenburg Counties. A combination freight and passenger station was located at Brodnax, shown here in a 1948 photograph. For many years, cotton was the chief crop in the region and the local Dugger Cotton Company had the largest cotton market in Virginia. The Brodnax Cotton Mill was also located in the town and bales of cotton were shipped from Brodnax by rail until the early-1950's. (William E. Griffin, Jr. Collection)

As the A&D was built through Southside Virginia in the late-1880's, a number of new towns came into existence, including Brodnax, LaCrosse and South Hill. The A&D was built through what would become the town of LaCrosse in the winter of 1889-90. On December 1, 1899, the Southern Railway, which had just leased the A&D, reached an agreement to permit the Richmond, Petersburg and Carolina Railroad (a predecessor of the Seaboard Air Line) to construct a railroad crossing at grade of the A&D at that location. The town of LaCrosse grew up around the crossing at grade of the two railroads and was incorporated as a town in 1901. In this 1948 photograph, we are looking east down the main line of the A&D at its crossing with the main line of the SAL. Note the derails on the A&D tracks just short of the crossing. To the left is the LaCrosse combination freight and passenger station that was built by the Southern Railway in 1926. This new station replaced the old A&D station that was destroyed by a fire on December 27, 1925. (William E. Griffin, Jr. Collection)

Located in the heart of Virginia's bright leaf tobacco belt, the town of South Hill has always been an important tobacco market. The town came into existence with the construction of the A&D. It was laid off and surveyed by the financiers of the railroad who bought 56 acres of land around the depot. The Southern built this new station at South Hill in 1924. Posing front of the new depot from left to right are Agent J. T. Pleasants, Operator F. W. Davis and Clerk A. M. Turner. (Shelby F. Lowe Collection)

After the Southern's new station was opened at South Hill in 1924, the town passed an ordinance requiring brick structures along Main Street. Hence, the Southern rebuilt the South Hill station to meet that requirement in 1927. It would prove to be the only brick station on the A&D. This photograph of the 1927 brick station was taken in 1948. (William E. Griffin, Jr. Collection)

The austere accommodations for passengers are clearly shown in this interior view of the South Hill depot waiting room. The photograph was taken in 1945 and the posters on the bulletin board exhorted travelers to buy war bonds. (William E. Griffin, Jr. Collection)

In the author's opinion, this photograph is one of the most delightful scenes he has ever found of a railroad station. We're are Boydton in the winter of 1948 looking west down the main line of the A&D. To the left is the Boydton passenger station and the separate baggage room building. To the right is the freight station where laborers are taking a break from their work. The pass track, which appears to have been freshly ballasted, and main line disappear in the distance. Every time I look at this photo, it makes me wish I could step into the scene to await the arrival of the next Southern Railway train. (William E. Griffin, Jr. Collection)

There's s sizable crowd, some arriving by horse and buggy, meeting the Southern Railway passenger train at Boydton in a 1920's-circa photograph. In the early-1900's, trainloads of vacationers came to spend the summer in Boydton at the Boyd Tavern, then known as the elegant Finch Hotel. South Hill Railroad Museum Collection)

By agreement with Southern Railway predecessor the Richmond and Mecklenburg Railroad, the A&D was given the right to operate over the 1.87 miles of the R&M RR between Clarksville Junction (shown here in a 1948 photograph) and Jeffress. The time tables, rules and regulations of the Southern Railway governed the operation of trains between these points. (William E. Griffin, Jr. Collection)

The Southern Railway had two stations in Clarksville - "Clarksville" on the Keysville-Durham line and "South Clarksville" on the A&D's Norfolk-Danville line. The A&D station is shown here in a 1948 photograph. When the A&D resumed independent operation in 1949, use of the "South Clarksville" name for the station was discontinued. This station was sold and moved to Roxboro, North Carolina for use as a restaurant. (William E. Griffin, Jr. Collection)

The Buffalo Junction station, shown here in 1948, was located in Mecklenburg County about 58 miles from Danville. The combination freight and passenger station was built in April of 1905 and served not only the passenger trains on the Norfolk-Danville main line but also those operating on the branch line from Buffalo Springs to the resort at Buffalo Lithia Springs. (William E. Griffin, Jr. Collection)

The house track siding at Nelson had a capacity to hold 24 cars. In this 1950's-circa photograph, only one A&D box car has been spotted for unloading. Fertilizer was shipped into Nelson. Pulpwood was handled both inbound and outbound from the station. (H. Reid Photo)

West of Nelson, the tracks of the A&D dipped into the state of North Carolina then re-entered the state of Virginia at Virgilina, a name derived from the town's location on the Virginia-Carolina border. This photograph of the Virgilina combination freight/passenger station was taken circa the mid-1950's. (H. Reid Photo)

Denniston, located at Mile Post 169, was an important agency station and interchange point for the A&D. There, the A&D interchanged traffic with the N&W's line from Lynchburg, Virginia to Durham, North Carolina. The agency was operated as a joint facility with expenses divided between the two railroads. The principal business at that location was the shipment of pulpwood to Union Bag Camp Paper, Continental Can and the Halifax Paper. This is a view of the A&D's Denniston station with the N&W station visible to the right at a lower level. The agency in the A&D's former Denniston station was closed by the N&W in 1963, after it acquired control of the NF&D, and agency functions were removed to the N&W station at that location. (H. D. Conner Collection)

For the first 30 miles east of Danville the main line of the A&D weaved its way back and forth across the North Carolina-Virginia border. The station at Semora, North Carolina, shown here in a 1940's-circa photograph, was built by the A&D in 1897. It survived until 1964, when the joint Semora-Alton agency was closed by the NF&D. (Ed Sharpe Collection)

East of Milton, North Carolina, the main line of the A&D left the river bottom and passed over hills until it dropped down to the Dan River near Jeffress. Milton was one of four water stations between Lawrenceville and Danville. Between those terminals, steam locomotives could take on water at South Hill, Clarksville Junction, Mayo and Milton. The Milton station and its water tank are shown in this 1948 photograph. (Old Smoky Railway Museum/Hampton Collection)

In 1949, the Southern Railway constructed a new diesel shop at Dundee in Danville to jointly service the new diesels that had recently been acquired by the Southern, the A&D, and Southern's affiliate, the Danville and Western. The new diesel shop is shown in this May, 1950 photograph. (Southern Railway Photo)

A&D RS-2 No. 101 is shown on the pit inside the Southern Railway's new diesel shop at Dundee in May of 1950. Work performed on A&D motive power by the Southern was charged to the A&D at agreed upon rates set up in contractual arrangements between the two railroads. (Southern Railway Photo)

CHAPTER 9

THE DIESELS FROM ALCO - PHOTOS AND ROSTERS.

ROAD NUMBER	BUILDER	MODEL	BUILDER'S CONSTRUCTION NUMBER	DATE	HORSEPOWER	ENGINE WEIGHT	TRACTIVE EFFORT
101	Alco	RS-2	76989	7/49	1500	248,910	62,225
102	Alco	RS-2	76990	7/49	1500	248,910	62,225
103	Alco	RS-2	77296	10/49	1500	248,910	62,225
104	Alco	RS-2	77297	10/49	1500	248,910	62,225
105	Alco	RS-2	77428	10/49	1500	248,910	62,225
106	Alco	RS-2	77429	10/49	1500	248,910	62,225
107	Alco	RS-3	78902	6/51	1600	247,500	62,225
1	Alco	RS-36	84119	10/62	1800	245,860	61,465
2	Alco	RS-36	84393	10/62	1800	245,860	61,465
201	Alco	RS-11	81459	2/56	1800	247,400	61,850
202	Alco	RS-11	81461	3/56	1800	247,400	61,850
203	Alco	RS-11	81462	3/56	1800	247,400	61,850
204	Alco	RS-11	81463	3/56	1800	247,400	61,850

Roster of A&D/NF&D diesel locomotives.

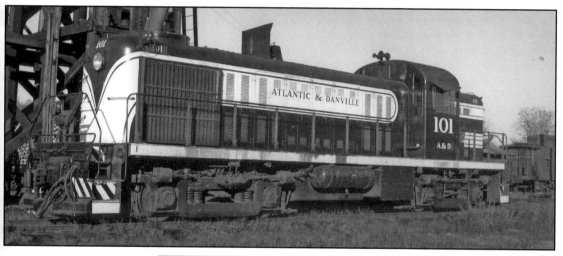

Six Alco diesel-electric locomotives were purchased in 1949 and a seventh was added to the roster in 1951. The first six diesels were 1500-horsepower RS-2's bearing road numbers 101-106. The first to arrive were Nos. 101 and 102 and they were immediately placed in service handling the A&D's new overnight service between Pinners Point and Danville. RS-2 No. 101 is shown at Lawrenceville on November 3, 1953. (Thomas Norrell Photo)

Having opened the switch to allow his train (the eastbound No. 70) into the side track, the head brakeman rides the front of RS-2 No. 101 into Franklin on March 10, 1959. No. 70 was taking the side track at Franklin for a meet with its counterpart, the westbound No. 69. (Mallory Hope Ferrell Photo)

A&D RS-2 No. 102 rests between assignments at Pinners Point in 1956. Both the 101 and the 102 entered A&D service in August of 1949 having been routed via Potomac Yard to the Southern Railway for delivery to the A&D at Danville. (L. D. Moore, Jr. Photo)

RS-2 No. 102 rolls across the main line of the Atlantic Coast Line at Boone Tower on a caboose hop from West Norfolk to Suffolk in 1953. (William B. Gwaltney Photo/C. K. Marsh, Jr. Collection)

A&D diesel-electric RS-2's Nos. 101-106 had 12-cylinder, 4-motor, turbo-charged engines. They weighed 248,910-lbs. and exerted a tractive effort of 62,225-lbs. The 103 is shown switching at South Hill. (Thomas G. Moore Photo)

RS-2 No. 103 and 105 ease A&D Train No. 69 past the Franklin station on March 10, 1959. (Mallory Hope Ferrell Photo)

A&D diesels were painted black with white striping. A freshly painted RS-2 No. 104 poses for the Alco company photographer in this builder's photograph. (Alco Historic Photos)

RS-2 No. 104 and RS-3 No. 107 have been placed on the ready track at Danville with their caboose in November of 1961 awaiting the arrival of their crew for evening run of Train No. 70. (Curt Tillotson, Jr. Photo)

Running repairs on A&D motive power were handled at Danville by the Southern Railway and at Pinners Point by the ACL. A&D locomotives were sent to Southern's Spencer, North Carolina shops for heavy repairs, engine overhauls and wheel work. In the latter period of the A&D's independent operation, the company also contracted with the N&W to perform repair and maintenance at its Roanoke Shops. RS-2 No. 105, shown here at Lawrenceville in July of 1960, reportedly outperformed all other A&D locomotives after an overhaul by the N&W at Roanoke. (William E. Griffin, Jr. Photo)

With the Hicks Street overpass in the background, RS-2 No. 105 backs down the main line into the yard while the train crew flags South Street crossing at the freight station. This photograph was taken in May of 1962. At that time, RS-2 No. 105 was one of the few A&D locomotives still in operating condition and by October of that year, the A&D would cease operations. (J. Parker Lamb Photo)

It was a rare sight to see three RS's units on a train. In August of 1956, RS-2's 106, 103 and 105 stop at South Hill with westbound Train No. 85 to set off the third unit to be used by the local. (James M. King Photo)

This view of a stored and unserviceable RS-2 No. 106 was taken from the bottom of the Lawrenceville turntable in May of 1964. I was never returned to active service. The N&W traded in the A&D RS-2's 103-106 and RS-3 No. 107 to EMD for new motive power (William E. Griffin, Jr. Photo)

The 107 was the A&D's only RS-3. This 1600-horsepower diesel, shown in this Alco builder's photo, was placed in service on July 1, 1951. (Alco Historic Photos)

The front of the long hood end of RS-3 No. 107. The diesel was at Danville in August of l962. (Curt Tillotson, Jr. Photo)

In August of 1962, RS-2 Nos. 101 and 102 were returned to Alco by the A&D and were remanufactured to become RS-36 Nos. 1 and 2. The 102 had been removed from service on December 16, 1958 and the 101 on February 11, 1960. However, by the time the new low-nose 1800-horsepower RS-36's were delivered, the A&D had ceased to exist. These last A&D locomotives, the 1 is shown here in an Alco builder's photo, were not delivered until October 1, 1962 - a month after the A&D had been sold to the N&W and reorganized as the NF&D. (Alco Historic Photos)

The paint scheme for the long hood end of the RS-36 is shown in this view of No. 2 taken at South Hill in October of 1964. The new RS-36 was photographed with RS-3 No. 107 that has already been stenciled for the NF&D. (James M. King Photo)

The front of the short hood end of RS-36 No. 2. The diesel was at Danville in November of 1962. (Curt Tillotson, Jr. Photo)

Following the acquisition of the A&D by the N&W, three of the RS-2's (Nos. 103, 104 and 105) retained their numbers but were stenciled on the cab sides for the NF&D. The A&D's name was also removed from the locomotive's carbodies. This photo of the re-stenciled RS-2 Nos. 104 and 105 was taken at Lawrenceville in 1964 while the diesels were parked next to the enginehouse. (William E. Griffin, Jr. Photo)

RS-2 No. 103 was repainted in 1966 with the solid blue paint scheme then being applied to N&W locomotives. It was the only former A&D RS-2 to receive this paint scheme. The locomotive also sports the dual sealed beam head lights that were applied to the A&D RS-2's by the N&W shops in 1964. This photo of the 103 in its new blue paint scheme was taken at Lawrenceville in April of 1967. (William E. Griffin Jr. Photo)

The A&D's RS-36's were repainted black, first with gold and later with white striping and lettering. Affectionately known to the NF&D employees and railfans as the "Ace" and the "Deuce", they were usually operated with the long-hood end facing west. These two locomotives served the NF&D admirably for many years, working in concern with RS units such as RS-11 No. 203 at Suffolk on April 10, 1977. The "Ace" was retired on June 27, 1980 and sold to Naparano Iron and Metal, New Jersey, on October 20, 1980. This left the "Deuce" with the distinction of remaining in service longer than any other A&D/NF&D locomotive. It was finally retired on March 21, 1984 and was subsequently donated by the N&W to the Tidewater Chapter of the National Railway Historical Society. Pursuant to an arrangement with the NRHS chapter, the locomotive has been used in operations on the Delaware Valley Railroad. (Bob Graham Photo)

The Alco tradition of the A&D was continued during the NF&D era. When the RS-2's were retired, the N&W sold four former Nickle Plate Railroad RS-11's to the NF&D. They came to the NF&D as follows: No. 201 (December 31, 1966); No. 202 (January 1, 1967); No. 203 (June 8, 1967); and No. 204 (June 3, 1967). These locomotives had come to the N&W following its merger with the NKP, were surplus to the system's requirements, and came to the NF&D through an intra-company arrangement. RS-11 No. 201 is at Suffolk in 1975. (Tom L. Sink Photo/C. K. Marsh Jr. Collection)

RS-11 No. 201 arrives at Lawrenceville running long hood forward with a small local freight in April of 1970. The RS-11's were powered with a 12-cylinder, 1800-horsepower, 251-B model Alco engine. (Stanley W. Short Photo)

With deep notches in the hood ends, an intercooler radiator hanging down on the side of the hood near the radiator shutters, and carbody filters spaced along the top of the long hood, the NF&D Nos. 201-204 were typical RS-11's. In fact, as NKP units, these engines were first production RS-11's. They were the fourth, sixth, seventh and eighth RS-11's built by Alco. RS-11 No. 202 is shown with its train at Suffolk on July 2, 1972. (Tom L. Sink Photo)

RS-11 No. 202 heads up a motive power consist that also includes N&W T-6 No. 44 and another NF&D RS-11 to roll an eastbound freight on the mainline east of Lawrenceville. (Ed Sharpe Photo)

When delivered to the NF&D, the RS-11's were painted in the N&W blue paint scheme with white lettering and striping. Later, they were repainted black. The NF&D herald and road number were located on the side of the cab. No heralds or lettering were located on the carbody or ends of the hoods. Perhaps the kindest description of these units is that they were utilitarian locomotives. They were always dirty with their paint flaked away and frequently - as was the case with No. 203 shown here at Courtland on April 12, 1977 - their heralds and striping were almost nonexistent. However, what they lacked in aesthetics they more than made up for in performance, serving the NF&D well until retired in the early 1980's. (Tom L. Sink Photo)

NF&D Train No. 85 arrives at the Danville yard with a 41-car train led by NF&D RS-11 No. 204, N&W T-6 No. 34 and NF&D RS-11 No. 201 on the morning of June 21, 1980. The RS-11's are in their final days of service. Nos. 202 and 203 were retired from service on June 27, 1980 and were sold for scrap. No. 204 was retired on July 21, 1981 and No. 201 was retired on July 21, 1982. They were both traded-in to GE by the N&W for new motive power. (Curt Tillotson, Jr. Photo)

CHAPTER 10

A&D/NF&D ROLLING STOCK - PHOTOS AND EQUIPMENT REGISTERS.

The A&D began independent operations in 1949 with fifty-eight former Southern Railway SU-class 36-foot boxcars. Numbered 500-557, they were double-sheath (wood-sided) with truss rods and a steel center-sill, ends and roof. The Southern Railway owned over 15,000 of these boxcars and they were operated over the A&D by the Southern from 1922 until the end of the lease. This view of No. 524, which was used as the A&D's express car for a number of years, was taken at Suffolk in April of 1950. (H. Reid Photo)

Tobacco was shipped in 1,100-pound hogsheads. With a forklift truck, the A&D could load a 36-foot boxcar in about 45 minutes with 40 hogsheads to a car. A&D boxcar No. 511, shown being loaded with tobacco at Danville, was converted into A&D wood rack car No. 1079 in 1953. (William E. Griffin, Jr. Collection)

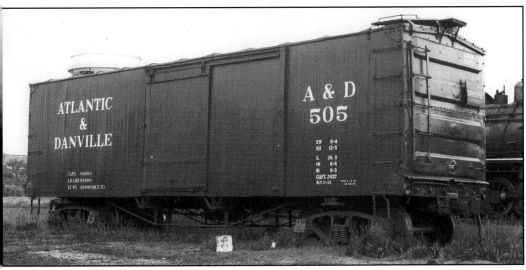

This view of A&D boxcar No. 505 provides an excellent view of the car's modified Hutchins end with the fascia removed. Some the A&D 36-foot boxcars retained the fascia until they were rebuilt into maintenance of way or pulpwood cars. None of the 36-foot boxcars were equipped with AB brakes and all were out of revenue service by 1954. (Thomas Norrell Photo)

The A&D acquired its first all-steel boxcars when it purchased 25 (Nos. 2001-2025) regular 40'6" 80,000-pound capacity boxcars from Ortner Company of Cincinnati, Ohio in 1954. The boxcars were originally owned by the New York Central Railroad and were rebuilt for the A&D by Ortner during August and September of 1954. (Bob Lorenz Collection)

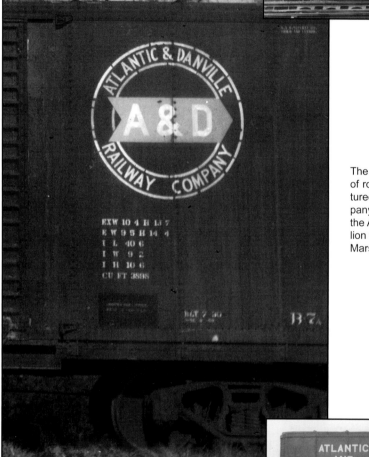

The A&D boxcars in the number series 2001-2025 were also the first pieces of rolling stock to receive the distinctive A&D medallion. The medallion featured an arrow that was painted a light blue color (Sherwin Williams Company paint # 152) and it corresponded to the medallion then being used on the A&D's Traffic Department letterhead stationary. This photo of the medallion was taken of a B7a class A&D boxcar of the 2200 number series. (C. K. Marsh, Jr. Collection)

The A&D continued to add to its fleet of all-steel boxcars and in 1957, one hundred 100,000-pound capacity class B7a boxcars were acquired from the N&W. The cars were stenciled "N&W Railway Owner and Lessor". (W. C. Whittaker Photo)

The A&D also purchased a group of ex-BS-class boxcars from the N&W. These were double-door boxcars on the N&W but were modified with a single door for the A&D, becoming its 2100-series. Note the new panel that has been added to No. 2169 creating a single door boxcar. This photo of the 2169 was taken at Lawrenceville on April 24, 1960. (Lloyd Moore Photo/C. L. Goolsby Collection)

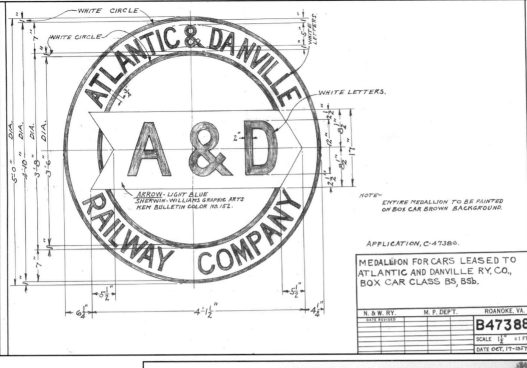

Stencil prepared by the N&W of the A&D medallion for the Class BS boxcars. (Fred Mullins/Russell Underwood Collection)

The only double-door A&D boxcars were a group of ex-N&W BS cars, numbered in the 2300 series by the A&D. This photo of the 2320 was taken on July 2, 1959 when the car was off line at Erwin, Tennessee. (Bob's Photo/Fred Mullins Collection)

In 1952 the Interstate Commerce Commission issued an order requiring that all freight cars used in interchange service be equipped with AB-type brakes by January 1, 1953. None of the A&D 36-foot boxcars had AB brakes and the railroad could not afford the costs of conversion. Since the 36-foot cars were rendered obsolete by this order, many of them were converted by the A&D into pulpwood racks or maintenance of way cars that would not be used in interchange. In this view, a group of 36-foot boxcars are shown being converted to maintenance of way cars at the Lawrenceville shops in July of 1953. (Ted Eudy Photo)

B&B Foreman S. E. Edwards supervises the conversion of 36-foot boxcars into maintenance of way camp cars at the Lawrenceville shops in July of 1953.   (Ted Eudy Photo)

The A&D also converted a group of its all-steel boxcars for maintenance of way service. Roadway service bunk car No. B-200 was originally A&D boxcar No. 2009, one of the original 40-foot steel boxcars purchased from the Ortner Car Company in June of 1954. The car is shown in roadway service at Franklin on March 12, 1964. (Tom G. King Photo/John C. La Rue, Jr. Collection)

While boxcars and pulpwood racks were dominant, The A&D also owned a few gondolas and hopper cars. The A&D owned ten 41'4", fixed-end, steel gondola cars numbered 3001-3010. These cars were ex-N&W GU-class cars and were purchased by the A&D from the N&W on June 15, 1955. Gondola car No. 3003 was photographed at Lawrenceville. (D. Courtney Griffin Photo)

The A&D also owned two 36'9", 3-bay, 70-ton steel hopper cars. Numbered 4001-4002, these were ex-N&W class H-3 hopper cars. The 4001 was photographed at Lawrenceville in June of 1962. (Tom G. King Photo/C. K. Marsh, Jr. Collection)

Beginning in 1940, the Southern Railway began rebuilding its surplus SU-class 36-foot boxcars into open pulp rack cars, eventually converting 2,860 of these boxcars for pulpwood service. Ownership of 39 of these cars was transferred to the A&D when the Southern Railway terminated its lease of the railroad. They were renumbered into the A&D 1000-1067 series. This photo of a loaded No. 1020 (ex-Southern No. 124582) was taken at Lawrenceville. (D. Courtney Griffin Photo)

A&D open pulp rack car No. 1028 (photographed at Boydton) was formerly Southern 114615 and was rebuilt from a Murphy-end box car which was originally built in 1926. Note that the diagonal member is wider since it is not "L"-bar stock. Also, notice the reinforcing plates placed over the truck bolster area and the "I"-beam supporting the queen posts. (Thomas G. Moore Photo)

This 1949 photograph shows a typical A&D freight near Jeffress, running behind loaned Southern Railway Ks-class 2-8-0 No. 682, with a group of empty wood rack cars in the consist. The closest car is A&D No. 1057 with original bracing (none of which is "L" shaped). The next car is a modified Southern car with "L" diagonal and vertical bracing. The third and fourth woodracks are Southern unmodified cars with the closer one having "L" diagonal bracing and the other using flat stock. (Virginia State Library)

The A&D supplemented its fleet of pulpwood racks by contracting with Dunn's Marine Railway Company of West Norfolk to convert a number of its 36-foot boxcars into open rack cars. The loaded No. 1093 was built from a converted A&D 36-foot SU boxcar. (H. Reid Photo)

There were over 2-million acres of pulpwood timber in the area served by the A&D. Lumber and lumber products were hauled by the railroad from many towns along its line. Much of this pulpwood was transported to Franklin for the large paper mills of Camp Manufacturing, St. Regis Paper Company and Taggart Paper Bag Company. Pulpwood rack No. 1140, a 43-foot car with steel ends and floors, was photographed at Lawrenceville in April of 1967. It was one of three (Nos. 1138-1140) ex-"F2"-class cars acquired from the N&W. (Tom G. King Photo/C. K. Marsh Jr. Collection)

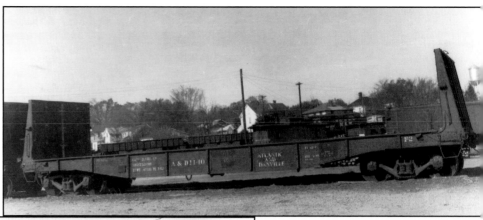

The A&D also owned thirty-seven (Nos. 1101-1137) ex-N&W class "FD" 35-foot woodracks with steel ends and floors. This view of No. 1110 was taken at Lawrenceville in October of 1962. (Tom G. King Photo/C. K. Marsh, Jr. Collection)

The A&D had little use for flatcars other than company service. Four 40-foot ex-Southern Railway flatcars (Nos. 801-804) were transferred to the A&D at the termination of the lease. They had steel fishbelly underframes and side sills with a wooden deck. Nos. 802 and 803 were sold to Camp Manufacturing in 1950. No. 801 was photographed in company service at Franklin on March 28, 1964. (John C. La Rue, Jr. Collection)

The A&D began independent operation in 1949 with nine ex-Southern Railway 37-foot, wood, 4-side window, center cupola cabooses. The A&D caboose cars were numbered X-100 to X-108, inclusive and were ex-Southern Railway caboose car Nos. X-1796, X-2041, X-2394, X-2027, X-2711, X-2046, X-2268, X-2712 and X-2708, respectively. The X-100 was photographed at Suffolk in March of 1954. (August A. Thieme, Jr. Photo)

The wooden cabooses were painted red with black roof and yellow lettering as was the style of their former owner, the Southern Railway. The X-104 was destroyed in a derailment at M. P. 109.9 on December 12, 1952. The X-100 had its trucks removed in 1961 and was converted to a yard building for use at Lawrenceville. The other former Southern Railway cabooses were all retired by the early 1960's. The X-108 was photographed at Suffolk on March 14, 1949. (H. Reid Photo)

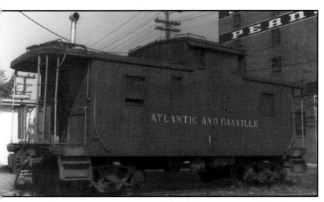

By 1961, most of the ex-Southern Railway wood cabooses were in poor mechanical condition and the A&D had to supplement its fleet by purchasing two cabooses from the N&W. Nos. 1 and 2 were both N&W CF-class caboose, with a steel underframe and sheathed in wood. These cabooses had no windows in the ends of the body and the small third window was found on only one side of the car. A&D No. 1 was photographed at Suffolk in September of 1964. (Tom G. King Photo/C. K. Marsh, Jr. Collection)

he A&D never owned a steel body caboose. As more of the ex-outhern Railway cabooses were retired from service, the A&D cquired three more second-hand 34-foot wood sheathed cabooses the 109, 110 and 111. The 111 is shown at Franklin on March 28, 964. (John C. La Rue, Jr. Collection)

THE ATLANTIC AND DANVILLE RAILWAY COMPANY.

SEABORN J. FLOURNOY, Trustee

GENERAL OFFICERS.

. D. CURTIS, Chief Executive Officer to Trustee............Norfolk 10, Va. | W. FRED BONNEY, JR., General Traffic Manager..............Norfolk 10, Va.

GENERAL OFFICES, 115 WEST TAZEWELL ST., NORFOLK 10, VA.

Miles of road operated, 205; gauge 4 ft. 8½ in. Locomotives (diesel electric), 7.

FREIGHT EQUIPMENT.—Reporting Marks—"A D"

The freight cars of this Company are marked "The Atlantic and Danville Ry. Co." and "A & D Ry. Co." and numbered and classified as follows:

This listing from the January, 1962 edition of the Official Railway Equipment Register shows the rolling stock of the A&D in its last year of independent operation.

FREIGHT CONNECTIONS AND JUNCTION POINTS.

Jan., 1962.

NORFOLK, FRANKLIN AND DANVILLE RAILWAY COMPANY.

4   THE OFFICIAL RAILWAY EQUIPMENT REGISTER

W. G. BLADES, General Manager.....................Suffolk, Va.

GENERAL OFFICES, 181 SOUTH MAIN STREET, SUFFOLK, VA. 23434

Miles of road operated, 205; gauge 4 ft. 8½ in. Locomotives (diesel electric), 6.

FREIGHT EQUIPMENT.—Reporting Marks—"A D" and "N F D"

The freight cars of this Company are marked "The Atlantic and Danville Ry. Co." and "A & D Ry. Co." or "N F D" and numbered and classified as follows:

ne NF&D owned 223 cars (the most ever on its ster) when its rolling stock was listed in the January, 1970 edition of the Official Railway Equipment egister.

FREIGHT CONNECTIONS AND JUNCTION POINTS.

Jan., 1970.

A portion of the capital the N&W committed to the improve the operating equipment of the NF&D was spent on the acquisition of dependable, revenue producing freight cars. In 1967, the N&W arranged for the NF&D to purchase 200 ex-Nickle Plate 50-foot, 50-ton double door boxcars. The cars were rebuilt at the N&W' Decatur shops and were assigned numbers in NF&D series 2300-2499. When delivered, the cars carried a 30-inch tall version of the slated NF&D logo that had been previously applied to the locomotives and were painted boxcar red with white stenciling. Beginning in 1974, some of these cars were repainted black with white lettering. Some repainted cars retained the logo and spelled-out road name. Others, such as the 236 shown here at Suffolk on February 21, 1983, only displayed the reporting marks and car data to the left of the doors. (William E. Griffin, Jr. Photo)

The original boxcar red paint scheme with white logo, road name and stenciling is shown in this side view of NF&D boxcar No. 2406. (William E. Griffin, Jr. Collection)

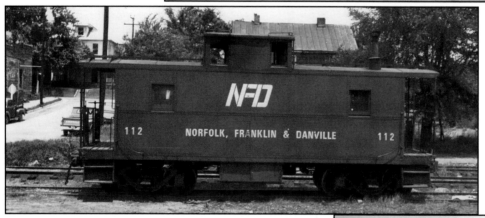

While many N&W cabooses were operated on NF&D trains, the NF&D did own two all steel cabooses numbered 112 and 113. Obtained from parent N&W, they were 36-foot CG class cabooses. The 112 awaits its next call to service at Lawrenceville on May 9, 1964. (Warren Calloway Collection)

NF&D caboose Nos. 112 and 113 were painted red with white lettering. The 113 had a fresh paint job when photographed in the Lawrenceville yard in August of 1963. (William E. Griffin, Jr. Photo)

In a classic photo of A&D operations, RS-2 No. 105 leads an eastbound freight train as it arrives at Franklin, Virginia on July 5, 1962. A few months later, in September of that year, the A&D would cease operations. The line would be purchased by the Norfolk and Western Railway and would continue operations as the Norfolk, Franklin and Danville. Adding Franklin to the railroad's name was a recognition of the importance of the shippers located at that point. The frame station shown in this photo would be demolished in June of 1963 and replaced by the only new station to be built on the NF&D. But in the summer of 1962, Bill Gwaltney was in Franklin to record this classic view of the A&D in the final days of its operations. (William B. Gwaltney Photo)

H. Reid framed Southern Railway Ks-Class 2-8-0 No. 726 under the branches of a nearby pine tree as the little Consolidation rolls a heavy freight train across the wooden trestle at Eastover near Suffolk. The photo was taken in the summer of 1949, shortly before the A&D resumed independent operations. (H. Reid Photo)

The line between West Norfolk and Suffolk provided H. Reid with many excellent locations to photograph the operation of Southern Railway steam locomotives on the A&D. On June 11, 1949, Reid and Bill Gwaltney chased Southern Railway Ks-Class 2-8-0 No. 739 with its little freight train enroute to Suffolk. Here the 739 is shown at Eastover as its nears the end of its run to Suffolk. (H. Reid Photo)

A Southern Railway freight from West Norfolk nears Boone behind Ks-Class 2-8-0 No. 723 in the summer of 1949. (H. Reid Photo)

Flying the flags of an extra, A&D RS-2 No. 102 is shown on a caboose hop enroute to Pinners Point. The train has just passed Boone Tower and is traveling eastbound on ACL tracks between Boone and Pinners Point. The train is just passing the semaphore signal governing the approach of westbound trains. In the distance to the right of the train, just over the trees, is the semaphore signal governing the approach of trains from West Norfolk on the A&D line to Suffolk. This photograph was taken in September of 1949 shortly after the A&D commenced independent operation of its line. (William B. Gwaltney Photo)

A&D RS-2 No. 106 is at Pinners Point in August of 1958. Delivered in September of 1949, this diesel had 1500-horsepower and was one of six RS-2 type locomotives purchased by the A&D from Alco. (William B. Gwaltney Photo)

In June of 1951, the A&D purchased its only 1600-horsepower RS-3 (No. 107) from Alco. The 107 is shown here along with RS-2 No. 104 as it switches an industry at Courtland in May of 1962. (William B. Gwaltney Photo)

In an action view taken from track level, RS-3 No. 107 and RS-2 No. 104 are shown arriving Courtland with their train in May of 1962. (William B. Gwaltney Photo)

During its later years of operation, the A&D's diesels were frequently out of service for repairs and the railroad was required to lease locomotives from other railroads to operate its trains. In this photo, Chesapeake and Ohio Railway S-2 No. 5007 is shown with the eastbound West Norfolk local at Boone Tower in March of 1959. (William B. Gwaltney Photo)

A&D RS-36 No. 1 was still stenciled for the Atlantic and Danville when photographed at Franklin on July 1, 1963. However, by that date the A&D had ceased to exist. The two RS-36's were not delivered to the property until October 1, 1962 - a month after the A&D had been sold to the N&W. (William B. Gwaltney Photo)

This excellent view of the long hood end of RS-36 No.1 was taken at Suffolk in March of 1964. (Carl Overstreet Photo/Russell Underwood Collection)

An A&D eastbound freight passes the Suffolk freight station after crossing Washington Street in 1952. The ACL's passenger station was located on the opposite side of the Washington Street crossing on the same side of the tracks as the A&D station. (H. Reid Photo)

The A&D Conductor positions himself to receive any orders from the agent as his westbound freight passes the Courtland station in May of 1962. (William B. Gwaltney Photo)

The two-story passenger station at Lawrenceville was built by the A&D in 1899. The first floor of the building was used as the passenger station. The second floor provided offices for the Superintendent and Train Dispatcher. Southern Railway passenger trains ceased their stops at the station in 1949. This photo was taken in October of 1962. (Wiley M. Bryan Photo)

The Lawrenceville passenger station is surrounded by A&D rolling stock in this classic photo. In the foreground is A&D caboose No. 2 , a former N&W CF-class caboose. To the left, A&D 40-foot steel boxcars have been spotted in front of the freight station. (Wiley M. Bryan Photo)

The A&D combination freight and passenger station at Brodnax was sorely in need to paint when photographed in April of 1963. Note the separate "White" and "Colored" entrances on the west end of the building, which were typical of the segregated transportation facilities in the South during the period it served as a passenger station. Note also the A&D company sign on the crossbuck signal at the street crossing beside the station. (John F. Stith Photo)

The A&D inherited nine 37-foot wooden cabooses from the Southern Railway when it began independent operation. A&D caboose X-108, shown here at Courtland in 1958, was formerly Southern Railway X-2708. (H. Reid Photo)

A&D 34-foot wood sheathed caboose No. 109 was photographed at Suffolk on May 18, 1962. (H. Reid Photo)

A&D 34-foot wood sheathed caboose No. 111 was photographed on the westbound local at Franklin in August of 1958. (H. Reid Photo)

A&D class B7a 40-foot boxcar No. 2269 was photographed at Lawrenceville in June of 1963. (John P. Stith Photo)

The A&D's distinctive logo with its light blue arrow was first applied in 1954 to the railroad's initial order of 40-foot steel boxcars. (William E. Griffin, Jr. Photo)

For a number of years following the acquisition of the A&D by the N&W, the diesel locomotives retained their A&D numbers and paint scheme but were stenciled for the NF&D. In this photo, NF&D RS-3 No. 107 is shown with a freight train at Franklin on July 5, 1963. (William B. Gwaltney Photo)

NF&D RS-36 No. 2 is at Danville on August 13, 1967. The locomotive has received the NF&D lettering on its cab and the A&D's name has been painted over on the carbody. (Ed Fielding Photo)

In the early-1970's, the NF&D diesels were painted black by the N&W shops. That paint scheme was evident on a brilliant Fall day (November 15, 1979) when this NF&D eastbound freight rolled across the Seaboard Coast Line Railroad (former ACL) mainline at Emporia. Motive power was provided by NF&D RS-36 No. 2, N&W T-6 No. 46 and NF&D RS-11 No. 204.   (William G. McClure Photo)

When the former A&D RS units were retired, the NF&D acquired four former Nickle Plate Railroad RS-11's numbered 201-204. In this photo, NF&D RS-11 No. 202 leads the eastbound NF&D local as it departs Lawrenceville in November of 1979. (Ed Sharpe Photo)

In a dramatic photo that perfectly illustrates the occasional undulating profile of the railroad, Jack Bruce photographed the eastbound NF&D local east of Emporia on June 30, 1980. Motive power is provided by NF&D RS-11 No. 204, N&W GP-35 No. 203 and N&W T-6 No. 49. (Jack Bruce Photo)

NF&D 50-foot, staggered door, all-steel boxcar No. 2473 is at Lawrenceville in 1969. (William E. Griffin, Jr. Photo)

NF&D caboose No. 113, shown here at Suffolk, was one of two 34-foot Class CG all steel cabooses. (William E. Griffin, Jr. Collection)

The author's mother watches the action as two N&W GP-30's, led by No. 543, lead the NF&D Local out of Lawrenceville on December 28, 1988. Motive power for trains on the NF&D was provided by N&W locomotives after the RS-11's were retired in the early 1980's. (William E. Griffin, Jr. Photo)

Norfolk Southern SD-40-2 No. 3260 sets out pipe in the Lawrenceville yard on June 8, 1996. This pipe was being delivered for construction of the pipeline to pump water from Lake Gaston to Virginia Beach, a project that was opposed by both Brunswick and Mecklenburg counties. When the pipeline was ultimately approved, delivery of the pipe resulted in a temporary source of revenue for the railroad. (William E. Griffin, Jr. Photo)

The last day for Norfolk Southern operation of the West Norfolk Branch was August 24, 1989. Perhaps appropriately, the motive power for the last train, shown here departing the chemical plant at West Norfolk, was provided by GP-38-2 No. 5172, still sporting a Southern Railway paint scheme. (Bill Schafer Photo)

Service on the West Norfolk Branch continues today as a result of the creation of the Commonwealth Railway, a subsidiary of Rail Link, Inc. Commonwealth Railway CF7 No. 517 is shown arriving West Norfolk with its train from Suffolk on August 15, 1997. (Russell Underwood Photo)